**Space, Time, Elements at
exactphilosophy.net**

Alain Stalder

Space, Time, Elements at exactphilosophy.net

Second Edition

Artecat

2021

First printing: 2021 (first edition: 2020)
ISBN 978-3-906914-09-1
Artecat Alain Stalder, Adliswil, Switzerland
artecat.ch

Contents

Introduction

My first contact with philosophy was when I was around ten years old. Me and my father were riding on a chairlift in winter and my father told me Plato's **Cave Allegory** with ants sitting in their earth and just seeing the shadows of the chairs of the chairlift cast into the snow in front of them. What would they imagine the world to be with shadows of skiers on chairs rolling by, one after the other?

I guess this relativizes the significance of any book, including this one. But still, this book represents some important advances regarding the slice of reality that humanity has cooked up so far.

Kant considered space and time things that exist a priori. While you can imagine space without anything in it, you cannot imagine anything without space a priori, and similarly with time. This brings me to my proposed novel approach to the world, to the immediate experience of living.

At the beginning there is just "**you**", the conscious mind that realizes it exists. It **sees** things; things outside, things inside the mind. (With "see", I actually include all senses, just easier this way.) And things move, they change their appearance or position, or whatever you might want to call it. These very basic experiences of the world already contain the essence of space and time: **Space** simply as what separates in and out and the different things there, **time** simply as movement or not.

This lead me in spring 2004 to consider to define "**elements**" in terms of pairs of opposites **in/out** and **rest/move**, i.e. in terms of space and time in immediate experience. More precisely, this yields four elements: One that moves outside, one that rests outside, one that moves inside, one that rests inside. I named the element that moves outside **emo**, simply for "**e**lement that **m**oves **o**utside", and so on. So there would be **emo**, **ero**, **emi** and **eri**.

As it turns out, these elements share some astonishing similarities with the four classical "Greek" elements **Fire**, **Earth**, **Water** and **Air**, as well as with the eight **trigrams** of the Chinese **I Ching** (Yijing). In this introduction I will only slightly hint at how this comes about; for details see the later chapters that were taken from my website exactphilosophy.net.

In **On Generation and Corruption** Aristotle bases his definition of elements on **touchable** properties of materials; wet/dry and hot/cold. He argues that wet/dry also includes soft/hard, malleable/brittle and smooth/rough. As it turns out, wet/dry resembles in/out in quite some ways. Things imagined inside are on average much more malleable by the will of the observing self than things outside.

I also define a fifth element, **e5**, as simply what transforms the four elements into each other. Again, I can show various astonishing similarities with how, for example, Aristotle defined a fifth element aether. I can even derive Aristotle's **circle of elements** in which elements transform into each other and relate it to e5, fitting also with Aristotle's notion that the fifth element would only move in circles.

Similarities are not based on Aristotle only, they generally match views on the classical "Greek" elements, and extend to other cultures, most notably to the eight trigrams Earth, Mountain, Heaven, Wind, Water, Lake, Fire and Thunder of the I Ching.

I can show that the trigrams can be arranged in a circle in which they would each stand for a transition between two "Greek" elements. For example, the Mountain trigram would stand for a transition from Earth to Fire and vice-versa, for hard rock from once molten lava, in contrast to the Earth trigram standing for a transition from Earth to Water and vice-versa, for soft sediments deposited by water. With **4 elements** you get **8 transitions in a circle**. Interestingly, and this is what initially gave me the idea, Richard Wilhelm had already noted in his book on the I Ching that the trigrams represent rather movement/change than things in their "state of being".

That arrangement in a circle is not identical to, but very similar to one of the two traditional ways of arranging trigrams in a circle, namely **Earlier Heaven**. The arrangement I discovered adds elements between trigrams, and arranged on a **Möbius Strip** its symmetries really **shine**, also combining the notion of in and out into a single cycle.

As somewhat of an aside, I also tentatively dive into the **prehistory** of elements, where there are some indications that there would have been first

3+1 elements based on the **colors of a fire**: **black** as coal, **red**/orange/yellow as flames and **white** as ashes. In the Indian Chandogya Upanishad these three colors are first associated with elements, synthetically all three as aspects of Fire and individually as Earth, Fire and Water. Imaginably something like a universal moon/sky goddess cult would have grown into the 4+1 classical elements. In any case, I provide some interesting new takes there.

But back to the core, back to elements defined in terms of in/out and rest/move…

Note that the present approach to elements is a priori **symmetric** with regards to in and out. This suggests that maybe there is not only a single outside world onto which all individuals look from their own angle, as commonly assumed, but maybe also just be a **single inner world**, also seen from different individual perspectives. In other words, inner individual worlds might be connected, share a common core, which reminds, of course, of Jung's **collective unconscious**. Also, since what is inside would tend to be soft and malleable, inside things might rather tend to **mix**, which would also suggest an internally interconnected world.

This could, for example, explain the existence of what Jung called **archetypes**, like that people dream similar things, including that themes from mythology keep turning up again and again even today. From there it is not far to astrology, where elements also play an important role, as all star signs are attributed an element. It is not the idea that contemporary astrology is caused by the "stars" out there, but likely rather that it is psychology, albeit **collective unconscious psychology**, thus affecting everyone, whether they consciously believe in astrology or not.

But that aside, contemporary descriptions of the star signs, especially in psychological astrology and most prominently in Liz Greene's **The Astrology of Fate**, mirror a transition between elements taking apparently place in all star signs. For example, the three Fire signs Aries, Leo and Sagittarius would involve different stages of a burning fire, from wood (Earth) via Fire to smoke (Air), or more abstractly from ero via emo to eri. The textbook astrology knowhow part of this is only very briefly explained in the main text at exactphilosophy.net reproduced here, so if you have no previous experience with astrology, it is probably not very accessible. But see the corresponding articles at exactphilosophy.net or my recent book **Elementary Star Signs**.

A core idea is that the **psyche** would think, feel, etc., essentially only **along** the circle of elements, and transitions between star signs for each of the four elements would lead inwards, where one would suspect the psyche. Now, as it turned out since the first edition, **Apuleius'** tasks of Psyche in **The Golden Ass** seem to be based more on Plato and following philosophies than anticipated. Moreover, also the archaic view of 3+1 elements can be understood in that view, and I can even derive heavy/light now, giving the core ideas critical mass.

Anyways, there is a whole lot of new ideas in what follows. Naturally, since the text is quite minimal and evolved in literally close to a million iterations over almost 20 years it is not something you can just read between breakfast and going to work. It is a book to **contemplate**, maybe on and off over a time span of years, a book to maybe take out into **nature**, far away from modern or postmodern disturbances, or at least to read when in the right mindset. But all this is, of course, entirely up to you.

The following is simply the core content of my web site, practically unchanged. To me personally it is also a work of **art**, so I even refrained from removing comments like "click here", which obviously won't work in a printed book. Well, if that was where you would already stumble, this book would definitely not be for you... ☺

If all else fails, simply visit the web site.

Maybe I will someday tackle the task to bring this in an even easier to access way to more people. Until then, this is it. To me personally, as a physicist, being very minimal is also a way to carve out the essential connections between things more clearly.

My approach to the world likely has the potential to grow into a new kind of science, likely close to what Kant had wished for for a future **metaphysics**, a kind of science a bit like today's physics, but with applications to way more areas.

Welcome

I present a way of looking at the world here. That way or idea is not something that can be proven. But some of the fruits it contains might be considered for tending to, grow and become part of existing systems of thought.

Just click sequentially through all menu items on the left, like reading chapters in a book, and take your time, or go to '  artemis' for every- and nothing. . .

I am a physicist (* 1966 in Zürich, Switzerland) and am doing this as a hobby.

Alain Stalder

way

After defining elements from immediate perception of the world, inspired by Kant and Schopenhauer, I relate these elements to physics, the ancient Greek elements, the eight trigrams of the Chinese I Ching, and more...

space and time

Imagine you just now started to look at the world.

One of the first things you notice is space. There is you and an outside world you can see, and you can see more than one thing. What separates you and what you can see, and what separates the different things you see, is space in its most immediate definition.

Then you also quickly notice that some things move and others do not. This is time, again in its most immediate definition, as motion or being at rest.

Things can rest or move outside and inside the mind. Thus there would a priori be 4 different kinds of things: What moves outside, what rests outside, what moves inside, and what rests inside. Let me call them *elements* and give them the following names: *emo, ero, emi* and *eri*.

emo	moves	outside
ero	rests	outside
emi	moves	inside
eri	rests	inside

leads

Some literature quotes, ideas and different points of view. Always also see '↝ artemis' for eventually articles that may expose some topics in a more contemporarily amenable way.

- A priori there is just an experience of being, which encompasses all that is. In that sense, space and time or the elements as tentatively defined above, may already be all that is. A conscious mind or self separate of the elements may a priori not be necessary, nor would it have to be limited to only part of the elements (like inside). But still some considerations related to an observing self further below.

- Immanuel Kant. *The Critique of Pure Reason.* 1787.

  In the early chapters, Kant discloses that some observable things cannot be isolated from the self, but instead appear to be themselves *a priori* necessary for thinking and observation. These a priori concepts include space and time in their immediate sense—the structure in which things appear in the mind and seem to exist outside of it.

- "By means of the external sense (a property of the mind), we represent to ourselves objects as without us, and these all in space. Herein alone are their shape, dimensions, and relations to each other determined or determinable. [. . .] Space is not a conception which has been derived from outward experiences. For, in order that certain sensations may relate to something without me (that is, to something which occupies a different part of space from that in which I am); in like manner, in order that I may represent them not merely as without, of, and near to each other, but also in separate places, the representation of space must already exist as a foundation. [...] We never can imagine or make a representation to ourselves of the non-existence of space, though we may easily enough think that no objects are found in it." (translated by J. Meiklejohn)

- "Time is not an empirical conception. For neither coexistence nor succession would be perceived by us, if the representation of time did not exist as a foundation a priori. [...] With regard to phenomena in general, we cannot think away time from them, and represent them to ourselves as out of and unconnected with time, but we can quite well represent to ourselves time void of phenomena."

- Arthur Schopenhauer. *The World As Will And Idea*. 1819.

  "[...] that the world which surrounds him is there only as idea, i.e., only in relation to something else, the conscious-ness, which is himself. If any truth can be asserted *a priori*, it is this: for it is the expression of the most general form of all possible and thinkable experience: a form which is more general than time, or space, or causality, for they all presup-pose it; and each of these, which we have seen to be just so many modes of the principle of sufficient reason, is valid only for a particular class of ideas; whereas the antithesis of object and subject is the common form of all these classes, is that form under which alone any idea of whatever kind it may be, abstract or intuitive, pure or empirical, is possible and thinkable." (translated by R. Haldane and J. Kemp)
  The word "Vorstellung" (for "idea") in the original means literally something "put in front of or before you".

- If I can imagine something, is it then really inside of me? Isn't there already a separation (space) between me and what I imagine? Such an extreme definition of *self* or *inside* would mean that the self cannot have any (consciously accessible) attributes, no memory etc., because any such attribute of the self would be something that can be considered by the self and would thus, by definition, not be part of the self...

- This definition of *self* reminds of the *Tao* ("way") in Taoism. Lao Tzu starts the *Tao Te Ching* with "The Tao that can be Tao'ed (trodden/spoken), is not the real (unchanging) Tao".

- In today's science, organs of perception wire back what is outside to the brain, where also mind and self would be. Maybe the self would even be considered "more inside than inside", looking out first at what else is inside and then even further out at what is outside. But how much of that is paradigm, and might thus change again over centuries?

- How would rest/move be defined for other senses than vision? How could eri and emi be measured inside? Would the only "objective" way be to measure brain activity outside? Would that be fundamental enough in this context? Could the self (observer) be measured?

- Would a female observer also consider what is seen as not being part of herself or would she rather tend to identify with what she sees? (Is the own body part of the self? And lovers, family, friends, house, garden, etc.?) In other words, is the distinction between in and out hard or soft (gradual)?

- What about sleep, dreaming, trance, drunkenness? Why only have a fully conscious observer?

metamorphosis

The next thing that one notices is that motion can start and stop, and that changes outside and inside seem not to be independent of each other. In other words, the elements change, maybe even metamorphose into each other.

What causes or allows these changes? Whatever it is, it must be something fundamental, like the four elements. So let me simply call it the fifth element, $e5$.

Free will seems to be a part of $e5$. It is possible to lift a spoon and then to throw it away, i.e. to get something outside that rests into motion ($ero \rightarrow emo$). However, free will cannot be identical to $e5$, as some things are much harder to control (try lifting a tree) and things transform all the time without conscious influence.

Freedom inside the mind seems larger than outside. It is much easier to lift a tree in the mind, than a real tree. But let me tackle things from a different angle: Outside on average more things rest than move, while inside the mind, things are almost always more flowing.

For example, a tree is at rest in most situations, except for a little movement of leaves and maybe branches. But if you close your eyes and try to imagine a tree at rest, it will get very hard after a few seconds not to deviate to other thoughts and to keep the tree at rest.

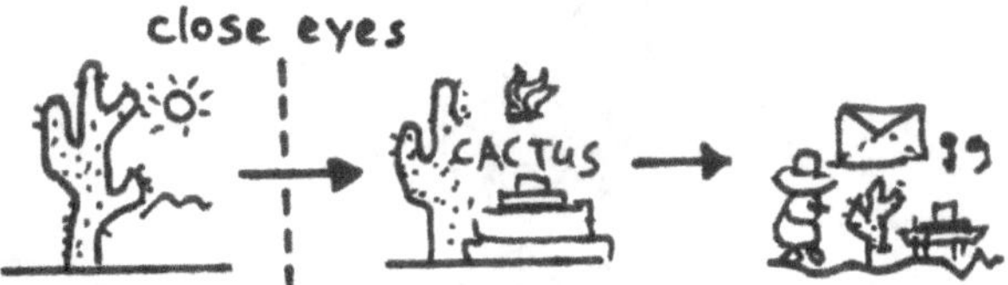

In conclusion, on average outside activity is needed to get things moving, while inside activity is needed to keep things at rest. More abstractly, emo and eri are thus active, ero and emi are passive. Also, what is outside resists motion on average more than what is inside. So emo and ero are hard (out), emi and eri are soft (in). What moves usually does so in various directions. Hence what rests appears to bind, what moves appears to release.

emo	moves	outside	active	hard	release
ero	rests	outside	passive	hard	bind
emi	moves	inside	passive	soft	release
eri	rests	inside	active	soft	bind
e5	transforms the above elements				

A camera can only register ero and emo, and thus only transitions ero ↔ emo, while transitions that would cross between in and out seem impossible. Personal experience might be a bit different, albeit a bit paradox, as follows.

If you leisurely observe a scene outside, like at the beach, usually most things will be resting, but there will be some movement. If you then close your eyes, in my experience, what will be immediately visible after closing your eyes will be the few things that moved, but frozen in movement, hence apparently a transition emo → eri, a transition in which activity is preserved.

Accordingly, passivity outside would then yield passivity inside, ero → emi. Actively created change outside, which more often means to get something in motion than the other way round, usually needs active focus inside first. Hence transitions in ↔ out would go both ways, emo ↔ eri and ero ↔ emi. Motion outside can also come to be and stop without much activity inside, like when an apple falls from a tree. Similarly, such things can also happen inside without much activity outside. Hence there would apparently also be transitions emo ↔ ero and emi ↔ eri. All in all, apparently a circle ero ↔ emo ↔ eri ↔ emi ↔ ero, while other transitions would at least be less frequent.

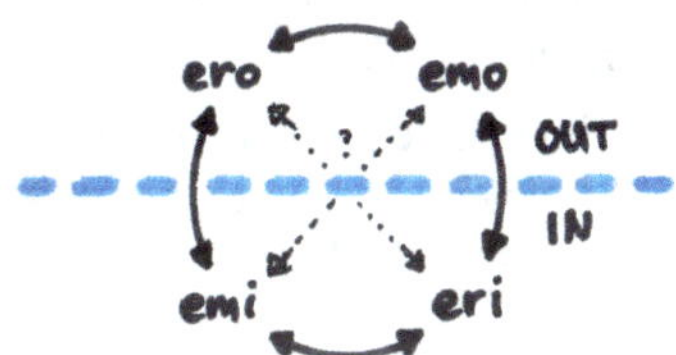

The elements could a priori interface in six ways: emo-ero, emi-eri, emo-emi, ero-eri, emo-eri, emi-ero. Any interface between elements must be unobservable, because otherwise it would be something that is perceived inside or outside, i.e. it would *be* one of the four elements. The same argument can be made for e5, of course.

Let me imagine an interface in-out as an infinitely thin membrane. And imagine, say, a blob of ero at the interface. If it remained passive, it could start to flow while permeating inside, becoming emi, or the other way round, and similarly for emo and eri.

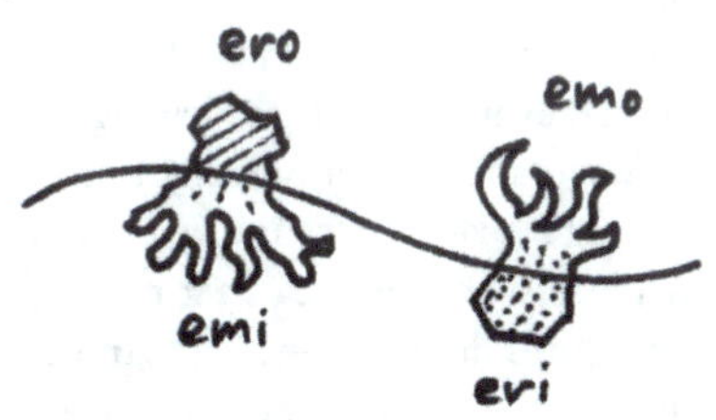

Since interfaces between elements would be invisible, just like e5, they might a priori have an arbitrarily complex nature, so that the above picture is a priori maybe just one of the simplest ways of seeing them.

leads

- If free will or the observing self is a part of e5, what is the rest? Cause and effect, fate, destiny, the free will of others, the own or collective unconscious? Quantum mechanics has relativized the first assumption somewhat, or maybe not.

- What property of the issue of free will or not leads to millions of variations when thinking about it? Could it possibly even be literally the effect of many "transformations" in the mind, even in circles, whatever that may mean precisely?

- Freedom to lift a spoon does not automatically mean freedom of choice whether to want to lift the spoon or not.

- The interface ero-emi could be seen as the arrangement of things outside related to a mood, a flow of feelings inside.

- When I say that outside more things rest than move, I mean this in a very specific sense: Relative macroscopic motion at time scales that human beings can register.
At long time scales, all things move; microscopically everything is in motion, as heat is nothing but random motion of atoms or molecules. When I turn my head, all objects move, but relative motion between them remains small.

- Some things outside keep moving, but often in a way "that rests by changing", reminding of Heraclitus, like a river that remains the same despite its water flowing, or often waves in the sea that move sort of periodically and only drastically change their average size and shape over longer periods of time than immediately observable. Fast moving clouds, however, can take on quite different shapes. And so on; all in all, categorizing outside as "hard" is not absolute.

- The present approach to nature is consequently centered on the human perspective, on direct experience of nature. Modern science usually differs from that by trying to pick a point of view from which a problem is easy to describe.

  The oldest example for this is astronomy that has been greatly simplified by solar centered calculations instead of using many arbitrary epicycles in geocentric calculations.

- Modern science is a very valuable companion for the present approach, especially for helping to exclude naive mistakes.

- Can my observations about motion, activity and hardness outside and inside be formalized and thus proven? How would such a mathematical representation look like? What assumptions would it be based on?

- In any closed system, *entropy*, roughly a measure of disorder, can at best remain constant, but usually it increases. With time, macroscopic directed motion and structures decay into microscopic random motion, which is, by definition, heat. Life manages to escape this fate by operating in *open* systems, by exporting disorder into the environment. That way, living beings can grow from microscopic seeds to complex structures and animals can repeatedly create directed motion.

  Since science considers the outside world to be mainly inanimate and the mind to be located in a piece of organic matter, the brain, it predicts that outside motion tends to disappear, while inside the conscious mind has a hard time focusing on something, because lots of mostly unconscious activity in the brain keeps stirring things up.

  Science is thus essentially compatible with the considerations presented so far, except for science's qualitative notion that creating motion inside the mind is active, requires energy, like outside. This might, however, simply be due to the viewpoint of science, which only considers facts in the outer, material world and might thus not be able to describe inner processes as experienced from the inside...

- In meditation, calmness of the mind (eri) is often sought by actively focussing the mind on something, thus reducing emi.

- In daily life, the outer world seems often bigger and stronger than the inner one. If you look at a bicycle and then close your eyes, you can quite quickly imagine the bicycle in your mind, but if you then imagine, say, that you add wings, and open your eyes again, you will usually not see a winged bicycle.

  Conversely, you can usually make everything outside disappear by just closing your eyes ("turn black", ero), or you can turn your head or walk away, so that the influence on what one sees outside is immediately very strong in that sense.

  Adding wings to a bicycle outside is still possible, but harder, because the outer world is harder. It requires several steps involving eri (planning, focussing), which then lead, via emo, to a different arrangement of ero, a winged bicycle.

- In *The World as Will and Idea*, Schopenhauer puts will before a distinction between subject and object:

  "[...] as feeling, a knowledge that his will is the real inner nature of his phenomenal being, which manifests itself to him as idea, both in his actions and in their permanent substratum, his body, and that his will is that which is most immediate in his consciousness, though it has not as such completely passed into the form of idea in which object and subject stand over against each other, but makes itself known to him in a direct manner, in which he does not quite clearly distinguish subject and object, yet is not known as a whole to the individual himself, but only in its particular acts,—whoever, I say, has with me gained this conviction will find that of itself it affords him the key to the knowledge of the inmost being of the whole of nature; for he now transfers it to all those phenomena which are not given to him, like his own phenomenal existence, both in direct and indirect knowledge, but only in the latter, thus merely one-sidedly as idea alone." (§ 21)

- There is usually less emo than ero and less eri than emi, but emo and eri are on average not disappearing. So transitions would have to be balanced and/or to return in loops.

  In today's science, the source of recurring activity would be the sun. The earth receives about the same amount of energy as light from the sun as it radiates back into the universe, which is why the temperature of earth is roughly constant. But since the earth receives energy from a single point in space and exports energy into all directions, it effectively exports entropy into space, thus preserving life on earth.

greek philosophy

Aristotle defines elements to be composed of properties that can be felt by touching. He uses two pairs of opposites, hot-cold and wet-dry, to define four elements, which he names *fire*, *earth*, *water* and *air*. And he identifies wet-dry with soft-hard, viscous-brittle and smooth-rough. Unlike later commonly the case, he does not consistently identify hot-cold with active-passive and light-heavy. If you do, you get a one-to-one correspondence to my previous definition of the elements in terms of in/out and rest/move:

△	fire	hot (active)	dry (hard)	emo
▽	earth	cold (passive)	dry (hard)	ero
▽	water	cold (passive)	wet (soft)	emi
△	air	hot (active)	wet (soft)	eri

Aristotle defines a fifth element as immutable, moving only in circles and existing only in space, while the other four elements move linearly. And he also arranges the four elements essentially in a circle in which they transform into each other by flipping one of hot ↔ cold or wet ↔ dry at each transition, while not completely excluding transitions that flip both at the same time, but considering them more difficult and slower. The shared theme of a circle links the transformation of elements to the fifth element.

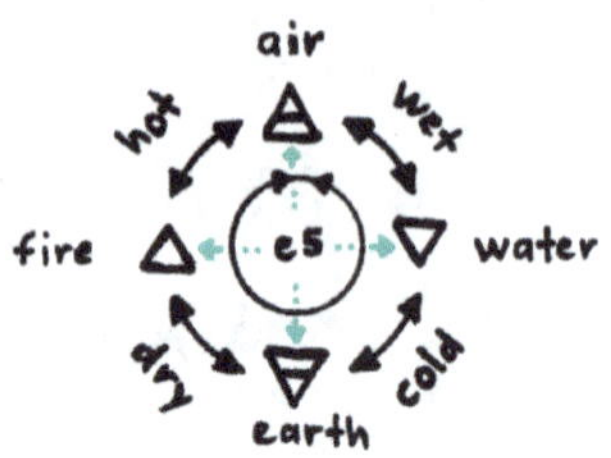

In other words, the same circle as tentatively derived earlier on from my definition of the elements, and a similar meaning related to e5, as also derived earlier.

Passive is inertial in a sense: Outside ero resists more to get into motion than emo resists to get to rest; inside emi resists more to get to rest than eri resists to get into motion. In rough equivalence to inertial and gravitational mass in physics, inert (passive) would be heavy and dense, swift (active) would be light and thin.

leads

- Aristotle. *On Generation and Corruption.* Around 350 BCE.

- "Since, then, we are looking for 'originative sources' of perceptible body; and since 'perceptible' is equivalent to 'tangible', and 'tangible' is that of which the perception is touch; it is clear that not all the contrarieties constitute 'forms' and 'originative sources' of body, but only those which correspond to touch." (Book II, translated by H. Joachim)

- "From moist and dry are derived (iii) the fine and coarse, viscous and brittle, hard and soft, and the remaining tangible differences. For (a) since the moist has no determinate shape, but is readily adaptable and follows the outline of that which is in contact with it, it is characteristic of it to be 'such as to fill up'. Now 'the fine' is 'such as to fill up'. For 'the fine' consists of subtle particles; but that which consists of small particles is 'such as to fill up', inasmuch as it is in contact whole with whole—and 'the fine' exhibits this character in a superlative degree. Hence it is evident that the fine derives from the moist, while the coarse derives from the dry. Again (b) 'the viscous' derives from the moist: for 'the viscous' (e.g. oil) is a 'moist' modified in a certain way. 'The brittle', on the other hand, derives from the dry: for 'brittle' is that which is completely dry—so completely, that its solidification has actually been due to failure of moisture. Further (c) 'the soft' derives from the moist. For 'soft' is that which yields to pressure by retiring into itself, though it does not yield by total displacement as the moist does–which explains why the moist is not 'soft', although 'the soft' derives from the moist. 'The hard', on the other hand, derives from the dry: for 'hard' is that which is solidified, and the solidified is dry."

- "The elementary qualities are four [...]. Hence it is evident that the 'couplings' of the elementary qualities will be four: hot with dry and moist with hot, and again cold with dry and cold with moist. [...] Fire is hot and dry, whereas Air is hot and moist (Air being a sort of aqueous vapour); and Water is cold and moist, while Earth is cold and dry."

- Aristotle arranges the elements in a cycle fire-air-water-earth: "Thus (i) the process of conversion will be quick between those which have interchangeable 'complementary factors', but slow between those which have none. The reason is that it is easier for a single thing to change than for many. Air, e.g. will result from Fire if a single quality changes: for Fire, as we saw, is hot and dry while Air is hot and moist, so that there will be Air if the dry be overcome by the moist. Again, Water will result from Air if the hot be overcome by the cold: for Air, as we saw, is hot and moist while Water is cold and moist, so that, if the hot changes, there will be Water. So too, in the same manner, Earth will result from Water and Fire from Earth, since the two 'elements' in both these couples have interchangeable 'complementary factors'. For Water is moist and cold while Earth is cold and dry–so that, if the moist be overcome, there will be Earth: and again, since Fire is dry and hot while Earth is cold and dry, Fire will result from Earth if the cold pass-away. [...] (ii) the transformation of Fire into Water and of Air into Earth, and again of Water and Earth into Fire and Air respectively, though possible, is more difficult because it involves the change of more qualities."

- In *On Generation and Corruption*, Aristotle considers light-heavy not to be an attribute of any specific elements:

"(i) heavy and light are neither active nor susceptible. Things are not called 'heavy' and 'light' because they act upon, or suffer action from, other things. But the 'elements' must be reciprocally active and susceptible, since they 'combine' and are transformed into one another. On the other hand (ii) hot and cold, and dry and moist, are terms, of which the first pair implies power to act and the second pair susceptibility."

But in *On the Heavens*, he considers air and fire as light and water and earth as heavy, in the order earth-water-air-fire, and postulates the existence of an immutable fifth element that dominates in the sky, is neither light nor heavy and moves in circles, while the first four elements move linearly:

"[...] all locomotion, as we term it, is either straight or circular or a combination of these two, which are the only simple movements. [...] Now revolution about the centre is circular motion, while the upward and downward movements are in a straight line, 'upward' meaning motion away from the centre, and 'downward' motion towards it. [...] For if the natural motion is upward, it will be fire or air, and if downward, water or earth. [...] circular motion is necessarily primary. For the perfect is naturally prior to the imperfect, and the circle is a perfect thing. [...] These premises clearly give the conclusion that there is in nature some bodily substance other than the formations we know, prior to them all and more divine than they. [...] there is something beyond the bodies that are about us on this earth, different and separate from them; and that the superior glory of its nature is proportionate to its distance from this world of ours. [...] things are heavy and light relatively to one another; air, for instance, is light relatively to water, and water light relatively to earth. The body, then, which moves in a circle cannot possibly possess either heaviness or lightness. For neither naturally nor unnaturally can it move either towards or away from the centre. [...] this body will be ungenerated and indestructible and exempt from increase and alteration [. . .] earth is enclosed by water, water by air, air by fire, and these similarly by the upper bodies" (Book I, translated by J. Stocks)

- Aristotle appears to consistently consider the pair of opposites hot/cold active and the pair wet/dry passive, see the quote from *On Generation and Corruption* above, or the following quote from *Meteorology*:

"All this makes it clear that bodies are formed by heat and cold and that these agents operate by thickening and solidifying. It is because these qualities fashion bodies that we find heat in all of them, and in some cold in so far as heat is absent. These qualities, then, are present as active, and the moist and the dry as passive, and consequently all four are found in mixed bodies." (Book IV, translated by E. Webster)

- In the outside world, the elements water and air (essentially liquids and gases or gas-like phenomena like clouds or smoke) appear softer and more fluidly in motion than the element earth (solid matter). The element fire (flames, lightning), however, does not appear to be visibly hard, while, like earth, quite closely related to dryness.

- While many works of Aristotle and Plato have been preserved in their entirety, works of earlier philosophers, as well of many later ones, like the Stoics, have usually only survived as fragmentary quotes by later philosophers, typically around early CE or even later. Since this was also the time in which the "canonical view" on the elements emerged for centuries to follow in astrology, alchemy, medicine, etc., it is difficult to reconstruct other views with certainty. Moreover, it seems that some schools of philosophy might have had oaths which would bind their members not to speak about certain fundamental views, or only in carefully veiled form.

In a nutshell, the earliest source I know of that attributes fire and air to active, and water and earth to passive is Cicero in *Academica* (45 BCE), possibly influenced by the Stoics. The first attribution of the same elements to male-female in astrology is Vettius Valens in *Anthologia* (2nd century CE). Aristotle names Empedocles at least twice as the first to have considered four elements. Plato introduces a fifth element in the *Timaeus*, most likely predating Aristotle.

A fragmentary closer look below and in following sections.

- David Sedley writes in chapter 11 of *The Cambridge History of Hellenistic Philosophy* (2000) that the Stoic's identification of fire and air with active emerged from medical tradition, from *pneuma*, breath, which was seen as a mixture of fire and air, and mentions also that this identification was originally not exclusively the only view of the Stoics in their time.

- In *Academica* (45 BCE), Cicero lets Antiochus of Ascalon say the following, influenced by Aristotle and maybe the Stoics: "Accordingly air [...] and fire and water and earth are primary; while their derivatives are the species of living creatures and of the things that grow out of the earth. Therefore those things are termed [...] elements; and among them air and fire have motive and efficient force, and the remaining divisions [...] water and earth, receptive and 'passive' capacity. Aristotle deemed that there existed a certain fifth sort of element, in a class by itself and unlike the four that I have mentioned above, which was the source of the stars and of thinking minds." (Book I 26, translated by H. Rackham)

- A bit later astrological views emerged that see fire and air as male, and water and earth as female. See Vettius Valens's *Anthologia* in the 2nd century CE and hints in earlier texts by Dorotheus of Sidon and Marcus Manilius. These views have essentially prevailed, including in medieval alchemy and up to contemporary astrology.

- In contemporary astrology, the element fire is associated with (visual) imagination and impulse, air with (abstract) thinking and communication, water with feelings and faith, earth with pragmatic realism—to give just a rough summary.

- Most things in the sky beyond clouds are round or cyclic: sun and moon are round; planets, as well as stars during night and seasons, move periodically in predictable cycles.

- The fifth element is also called ether or aether and quintessence. Many different views of the fifth element and closely related concepts have emerged over time.

  Plato used the word aether to describe the purest form of air in the *Timaeus.* But there is also a strong association of the sky with fire, because stars and planets appear to emit light and the sun provides heat, and also because fire was often considered the lightest of the four elements.

  The fifth element is generally considered "divine" because gods were often believed to live in heaven. And it is often also seen as special in other ways, like able to create life, or immortal like the soul or maybe pneuma, or able to create matter and to hold it together, or maybe identified by some alchemists with the philosopher's stone, which was believed to be able to transform matter, like lead to gold, etc.?

- Do such associations (historically founded or not) fit well with the definition of e5 simply because they all keep going in circles around the same questions?

- According to Diogenes Laërtius in the third century CE, the Stoics would have identified fire with hot, earth with dry, water with wet, and air with cold (and dry):

  "[. . .] the four elements are all equally an essence without any distinctive quality, namely, matter; but fire is the hot, water the moist, air the cold, and earth the dry—though this last quality is also common to the air. The fire is the highest, and that is called aether, in which first of all the sphere was generated in which the fixed stars are set, then that in which the planets revolve; after that the air, then the water; and the sediment as it were of all is the earth, which is placed in the centre of the rest." (7. LXIX, translated by C. Yonge)

The papyrus *Anonymus Londinensis* from about the first century CE says essentially the same about Philistion (apparently Philistion of Locri, a contemporary of Plato):

"Philiston thinks that we are composed of four 'forms', that is, of four elements—fire, air, water, earth. Each of these too has its own power; of fire the power is the hot, of air it is the cold, of water the moist, and of earth the dry." (XX 24, translated by W. Jones)

According to David Hahm in *The Origins of Stoic Cosmology* (1977), this view might have already been quite common among physicians in classical times. Artistotle's texts about biology seem to implicitly reflect that view, like that air is inhaled cold and exhaled hot (pneuma). Although there appear to be no contemporary sources that would directly prove such an identification, Hahm's detailed argumentation that the Stoics aimed for a unified view of the elements (unlike apparently Aristotle) across all fields seems plausible.

In Stoic belief, the cosmos emerged from fire via air to water to earth, and back (see Hahm for details), essentially along Aristotle's circle of the elements or light to heavy and back.

- In ancient Greek philosophy there was also the idea of matter consisting of indivisible physical units (atoms). In Plato's *Timaeus*, a model is presented that combines both views by associating the elements with the five Platonic solids: fire-tetrahedron, air-octahedron, water-icosahedron, earth-cube and the "roundest" one, the dodecahedron, for the whole world/universe (pan). Kepler's drawings (1619):

 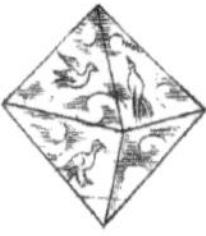   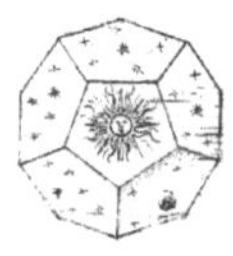

Today they are usually paired cube-octahedron, dodecahedron-icosahedron and tetrahedron-itself, because the centers of the surfaces yield the corners of the dual body.

In 4 dimensions there are 6 generalized Platonic solids, in 5 and more dimensions always only 3, namely generalizations of tetrahedron, cube and octahedron.

34

i ching

All cultures seem to know some kinds of elements, but let me consider the 8 trigrams of the Chinese Book of Changes, the *I Ching* or *Yijing*, which may be quite fundamental.

☰	heaven, strong, creative, father
☷	earth, devoted/yielding, receptive, mother
☳	thunder, inciting movement, arousing, 1st son
☵	water, dangerous, abysmal, 2nd son
☶	mountain, resting, keeping still, 3rd son
☴	wind/wood, penetrating, gentle, 1st daughter
☲	fire, light-giving, clinging, 2nd daughter
☱	lake, joyful, joyous, 3rd daughter

They seem to resemble Greek elements in pairs, namely heaven-wind (air), earth-mountain, fire-thunder and water-lake. Let me rearrange them into another table:

☰	heaven	**air**	rests	male
☴	wind/wood	**air**	moves	female
☶	mountain	**earth**	rests	male
☷	earth	**earth**	moves	female
☲	fire	**fire**	rests	female
☳	thunder	**fire**	moves	male
☱	lake	**water**	rests	female
☵	water	**water**	moves	male

Interestingly, the trigrams that correspond to the Greek elements, i.e. resting air and earth, moving fire and water, are exactly the male trigrams.

Let me map each trigram to the result of a transition between two elements in Aristotle's circle of the elements, ending with the corresponding element and starting with a male element (fire or air) for the male trigrams (father and sons) and with a female element (water or earth) for the female trigrams (mother and daughters):

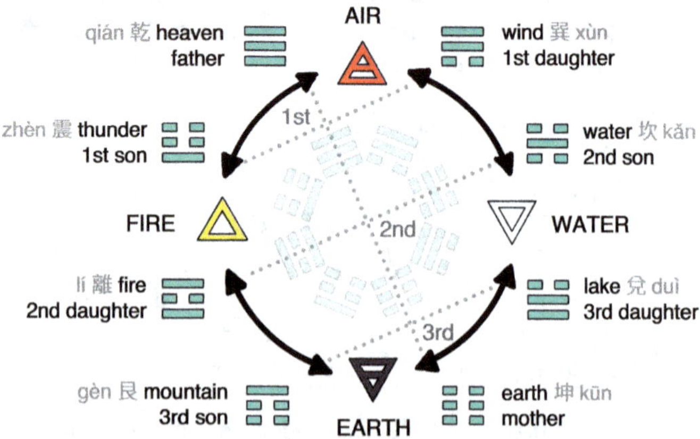

The trigrams seem to fit closely: Thunder as fire that has suddenly come down as lightning from the sky (air), in contrast to fire steadily clinging to the matter (earth) it burns; wind as air that gently evaporated from water, in contrast to gases from a fire risen to heaven; a lake as water sprung from sources (earth), in contrast to water fallen down as rain from the sky (air); a mountain as earth solidified from lava (fire), in contrast to softly yielding earth from sediments deposited by water.

☰	heaven	**air** ← fire	rests	male
☴	wind	**air** ← water	moves	female
☶	mountain	**earth** ← fire	rests	male
☷	earth	**earth** ← water	moves	female
☲	fire	**fire** ← earth	rests	female
☳	thunder	**fire** ← air	moves	male
☱	lake	**water** ← earth	rests	female
☵	water	**water** ← air	moves	male

This arrangement is none of the two traditionally known ones, more similar to Earlier Heaven than Later Heaven:

More symmetries, some similar to Earlier Heaven:

- Daughters and sons are arranged from father to first to second to third children, and finally to mother.
- Opposite trigrams in the circle mirror each other if you mirror each trigram at the middle line (i.e. swap first and third line) and invert all lines (yin ↔ yang).
- Trigrams that transform to or from outer elements have a broken (yin) line in the middle, which would fit with outer elements being harder and more brittle, breaking more easily.
- Excluding the middle line, between adjacent trigrams in the circle exactly one line is inverted (yin ↔ yang).

Let me arrange the circle of elements and trigrams onto a Möbius Strip ⊗ as follows (click for larger image):

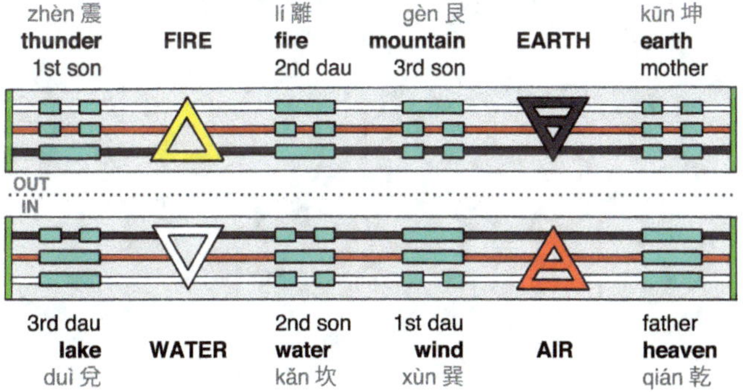

Inner elements are placed on the inside of the strip, outer elements on the outside. That way, the strip reminds of the supposed permeable membrane between in and out, but with different elements touching: The symbols for the moving elements fire and water touch on opposite sides of the strip, coinciding perfectly, and the same is true for the resting elements earth and air. All lines of the trigrams on one side of the strip are mirrored by their inverted lines (yin ↔ yang) on the other side, so that yin and yang *are* different sides of the same on the strip.

So, even though fire and water would touch, and maybe mirror each other between in and out, they could not transform directly into each other, only indirectly by going along the single surface of the strip via air or earth.

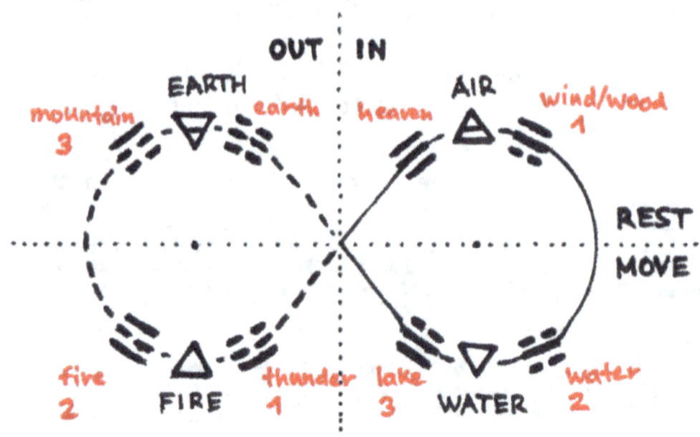

leads

- The I Ching is a divination system. By tossing coins or drawing yarrow sticks, one determines hexagrams (two trigrams) that are given meanings in the text of the I Ching. More precisely, the oracle results in two hexagrams, describing the evolution of the current situation to a new situation.

- This new arrangement of the 8 trigrams and 4 elements in a circle was inspired by a passage in the introduction of Richard Wilhelm's translation of the *I Ching or Book of Changes* (translated from German to English by Cary F. Baynes):

  "The eight trigrams are symbols standing for changing transitional states; they are images that are constantly undergoing change. Attention centers not on things in their state of being—as is chiefly the case in the Occident—but upon their movements in change. The eight trigrams therefore are not representations of things as such but of their tendencies in movement."

  So the 8 Chinese trigrams would express essentially the same elements and changes in a circle as the 4+1 Greek elements, i.e. the fifth element would be contained in the trigrams.

- Also in terms of bind/release, the trigrams seem to fit closely: Fire, heaven, lake and mountain hold their element in place; thunder, wind, water and earth let it go.

- No common historical roots are known, nor any roots of the above arrangement of trigrams in Chinese history, so did both cultures mirror nature independently, even unknowingly?

  Interpreting earth-water-air as the states of matter solid-fluid-gas and fire as a chemical reaction or physical phenomenon that produces light and maybe heat, the elements could be considered what is most commonly encountered in nature.

  The elements represent also *elementary* needs: air to breathe, water to drink, food to eat, sunlight and fire as energy.

  Conversely, the very nature of oracles is that things are connected, maybe also globally to some degree?

- Each trigram is part of 15 hexagrams. In the images of the hexagrams, the wind/wood trigram appears 10 times as wind, 5 times as wood or tree(s); fire 11 times as fire, two times as lightning, one time as light, one time as sun; water 11 times as water, two times as clouds, one time as rain, one time as spring well. The other trigrams appear as themselves.

- In the yarrow stalk method of consulting the I Ching, one starts with 50 yarrow stalks and initially puts one away. This seems to be a reference to the cycles of moon and sun, because 50+49 lunar months are only about 1.5 days short of 8 solar years, which is also why the Olympics in ancient Greece were held alternatively every 50 and 49 lunar months. Hence the moon advances about 3/8 of the circle every solar year, drawing an eight-pointed star over eight years, as well as appearing in eight different lunar phases.

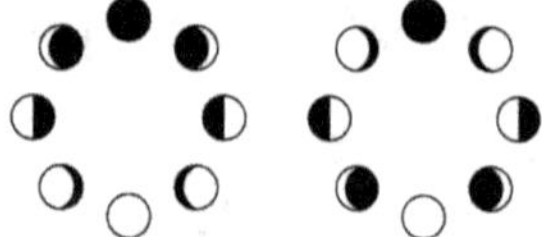

Venus never separates more than about 1/8 of the circle from the sun and appears to stand still 5 times in 8 years, drawing a pentagram that shifts only slightly between cycles. The Mesopotamian goddess of love Ishtar was associated with Venus, usually depicted as an eight-pointed star and sometimes shown together with sun and moon.

The yin-yang symbol ☯ reminds of moon phases.

"In its primary meaning yin is 'the cloudy', 'the overcast' and yang means actually 'banners waving in the sun', that is, something 'shone upon', or bright. By transference the two concepts were applied to the light and dark sides of a mountain or of a river." (Wilhelm/Baynes, introduction)

- The five Chinese Wu Xing, water, metal, fire, wood and earth, which are often called "elements" in the West, but literally mean "moving", stand most immediately for the five planets visible to the naked eye, Mercury, Venus, Mars, Jupiter and Saturn, while the "Four Symbols", black turtle (plus snake), white tiger, vermillion bird (phoenix) and azure dragon stand for the four directions and for constellations in the sky (each for a group of 7 of the 28 mansions). Together with the I Ching maybe standing for sun and moon, this would complete the sky and what it was believed to reflect down on earth.

- In the five Wu Xing, earth often has a somewhat central role, surrounded by things that emerge from it and go back to it: water from springs, fire from volcanoes, wood growing from earth and metal mined from it; four very useful ingredients for humans to shape their worlds, like using fire to smelt ore into metal tools, which can then be used to cut wood into houses, furniture, bows, plows, water wheels, etc.

- In the Chinese zodiac, four star signs are assigned to earth, arranged in a cross, and in the four sectors in between the two star signs there are assigned to water, metal, fire and wood, respectively. This reminds a lot of Aristotle's circle with trigrams above, so maybe the Wu Xing earth would correspond to the static Greek elements and the other four Wu Xing to the trigrams of the I Ching for the corresponding transformation? Can this be identified in the attributes of the star signs of the Chinese zodiac?

- Is the association of trigrams with elements and their changes also closely mirrored in the hexagrams and their changes?

- When consulting the I Ching as an oracle, the different lines are assigned the numbers 6 to 9:

6	old (changing) yin	- - to —	-x-
7	new (unchanging) yang	— to —	—
8	new (unchanging) yin	- - to - -	- -
9	old (changing) yang	— to - -	-o-

These numbers are also associated with the Wu Xing and

derived from 5 (earth) plus 1 to 4 (water, fire, wood, metal), see the Yellow River Map, e.g. in Wilhelm/Baynes.

As a different approach, let me number the elements in Aristotle's circle as 1-2-3-4, starting a priori with any element and going in either direction of the circle. Now, map transformations of elements to the sum of the three elements involved, $1+2+3 = 6$, $2+3+4 = 9$, $3+4+1 = 8$ and $4+1+2 = 7$, where the element in the middle is the one that is transformed.

This gives also the numbers from 6 to 9 and note that new yin and yang are obtained for the sequences that cross from 4 to 1, i.e. into a *new* cycle.

Let me number the elements 1-fire, 2-air, 3-water, 4-earth (starting with the lightest element according to Aristotle):

6	transformation of air	$36 = 6\times6$ Stratagems
7	transformation of fire	$49 = 7\times7$ Qixi (Ch'i ?)
8	transformation of earth	$64 = 8\times8$ I Ching
9	transformation of water	$81 = 9\times9$ Tao Te Ching

This fits astonishingly well with contemporary Western astrological views of the elements. The 36 Stratagems provide stratagems to use in politics and war, which fits well with air as conscious planning mind. The I Ching yields a priori images of changes in the outer, material world, the element earth, which are then interpreted in a more detached way. The Tao Te Ching, which comes in 81 sections, often has something that flows like water. Besides the 50/49 yarrow stalks, there is the Qixi Festival on the 7th day of the 7th month of the year when magpies mythologically build a bridge across the milky way to briefly reunite two lovers, and ch'i (qì) stands for life energy and breath (which reminds of pneuma), and is pronounced almost like the word for 7 (qī) in Chinese.

In ancient China, fields in agriculture used to be divided into squares of $9 = 3 \times 3$ fields, with 8 fields (earth) owned by individual families around a central 9th field that belonged to all families and contained the well (water).

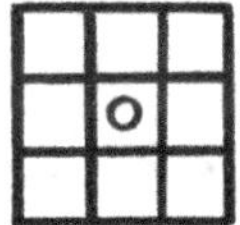

- The most ancient Chinese oracles used bones (typically shoulder bones of oxen) or turtle plastrons (the belly part of the turtle shell). Holes were drilled and heated with a heat source from the back of the plastron to produce cracks on the front, which were typically T-shaped. Although many oracle bones and plastrons have been found and the ancient writing can now be read to quite some degree, little seems to be known about how cracks were interpreted. There seems to be no direct evidence for an influence on the I Ching, so far.

A plastron consists essentially of 6 pairs of scutes (shields), anal, femoral, abdominal, pectoral, humeral and gular, with a flexible hinge between the first and the last 3 pairs of scutes, which reminds of the structure of hexagrams.

Applying heat to a plastron can cause it to crack, to become broken. Are yin and yang lines as broken (weak) resp. unbroken (strong) lines in the I Ching thus related to more ancient oracles involving heat?

Heat dries up, makes brittle, so would a yang line correspond to no crack emerging, because it was wet to start with, hence be considered strong in the sense of resisting heat?

On the northern hemisphere, stars appear to rotate around the north pole in the sky, the direction assigned to the turtle of the four symbols. Is the turtle with its shell maybe a model of the world, with the plastron standing for what is down on earth and the upper part of the shell for the sky? And similarly lower and upper trigrams of the I Ching? Would a plastron oracle have mirrored below what is above?

The hexagons on the upper part of the shell could be seen to form 6 unbroken/yang lines (heaven) and the pairs of plastron scutes 6 broken/yin lines (earth).

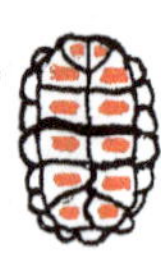

- See Billy Culver's *Energy Language* website, which inspired me once to reconsider old attempts to arrange elements and trigrams on a Möbius Strip ⊛ or an infinity symbol ∞ and whose style influenced the graphics above, but in my feeling his images carry more potential than that.

- Is the female fire trigram a form of inner fire, emo mapped to some form of eri, that is clinging to a dream, an idea, a wish despite all outer hardness? Is the female earth trigram a form of inner earth, ero mapped to some form of emi, something that can yield devotely to outer hardness? Is the female lake trigram a form of outer water, emi mapped to some form of ero, which brings calm to the outside world without hardness? Is the female wind trigram a form of outer air, eri mapped to some form of emo, free flowing mind and communication?

- Is the Chinese approach thus more balanced? Conversely, is the Greek approach more likely to start new things, exactly because it is maybe initially more imbalanced? Are both needed for 'full' balance? Is there more?

- In *Psychologische Typen* (1921), C. G. Jung combines extra- and introversion with implicitly the four elements, which he terms thinking (air), feeling (water), intuition (fire) and sensation (earth), into 8 psychological types, possibly already implicitly inspired by the 8 trigrams of the I Ching:

  "I first met Richard Wilhelm [...] in the early twenties. In 1923 we invited him to Zürich [...]. Even before meeting him I had been interested in Oriental philosophy, and around ["etwa"] 1920 had begun experimenting with the I Ching." (*Memories, Dreams, Reflections*, Appendix IV, recorded and edited by A. Jaffé, translated by R. and C. Winston, 1961)

Also in *Psychologische Typen*, Jung additionally categorizes thinking and feeling as "rational" or "judging", because they would judge the world based on their inside, and conversely intuition and sensation as "irrational", but even writes:

"But I am prepared to grant that we may equally well entertain a precisely opposite conception of such a psychology, and present it accordingly. I am also convinced that, had I myself chanced to possess a different individual psychology, I should have described the rational types in the reversed way, from the standpoint of the unconscious—as irrational, therefore." (X A III 5, translated by H. G. Baynes)

In that sense, what Jung calls "irrational" could also be considered "realistic", as judging the world rather based on measurement outside than on inner conceptions, just like in science, as opposed to e.g. medieval Christian views, where looking at Jupiter's moons through Galileo's telescope could apparently not have convinced people that not everything revolves around earth. In astrology, rationality is typically air, reality typically earth, but both air and water (which is usually considered rather irrational and related to the unconscious) have to do with judgment, which is maybe not so astonishing, considering that eri and emi would be inner elements.

So Jung would have been quite close in a way, with the first text I know of to bring "in/out" near "elements", with extra-/introverted and judging from within or without.

His definition of rational/irrational seems also to reflect the difference between medieval world views, where inner worlds had quite some weight, and newer ones, from the Renaissance on, where the outer world generally gained precedence.

- Love and happiness are felt inside, so maybe ideally not too much focus outside? Nor inside? But still sometimes? Or simply be with someone with a different perspective?

origins

It is my impression that a notion of first three "elements" and later '1+3', as opposed to four equitable elements plus a fifth element '4+1' as defined by Aristotle, may have been subliminally prominent throughout the ages long before recorded history and Greek philosophers.

In a nutshell, '1' would have become what makes things move, energy, fire, and '3' would have evolved to air-water-earth, the states of matter gas-liquid-solid. Colors would have been implicitly the light **green** of catkins and explicitly white–**red**–**black** in the order of a ripening mulberry, with roots in prehistoric cults around fire, and likely the moon, both as single creatress and in triplicity, world-wide.

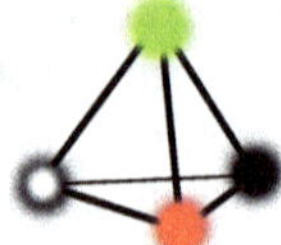

First named colors in virtually all languages were white-red-black as the colors of fire (light): **black** as dark, white as bright, and **red** as the colors of fire from flame to embers, yellow to red. Fire, humanity's first major discovery, would have initially been preserved in a raised mound of ashes (white) around a core of glowing coal (red around black). There would also have been cults around this, most likely a universal "white" moon/fire creatress/goddess. In ancient Greece sacrifices were given into fire and the first sacrifice always given to Hestia, the goddess of the hearth.

One of the earliest Indian Upanishads, the Chandogya Upanishad, which dates back to at least around 700 BCE, relates these three colors to "elements": red-fire, white-water and **black**-earth, probably also since water is more transparent (and hence "brighter") and ashes more "fluid" than earth resp. coal. It appears that at some point red became associated with air instead and the goddess came to represent fire and moon as the ruler of a triplicity of air-water-earth or sky, sea and underworld. Colors assigned to elements by Antiochus of Athens around the second century CE were accordingly yellow-fire, white-water, red-air and **black**-earth, and at least today's symbols are triangles.

Contrary to Aristotle's model, which is a priori based on touchable properties in the outer world, the present model involves also things inside the mind. In the outer world, emo and ero could be mapped via fire/earth to "energy/matter" and matter split up into its 3 main states.

Maybe inside, since 'states' suggests resting, emi could be '1' and eri could be split into 3 'states of mind', memory ('earth'), logical constructs including language ('air') and free imagination ('fire'), with increasing degrees of freedom similar to solid-liquid-gas ('earth-water-air') outside, yield-ing 8 'elements', similar to the trigrams of the I Ching?

See the section *psyche* for a simple tentative explana-tion of why first just three "proto-elements", **black** earth (ero), white water (emi), and red fire (eri+emo) of life.

leads

- Could three main states of matter outside be derived from the model or would that have to be added via experimental facts, like the observation that freedom inside seems larger than outside, which lead to passive/active, soft/hard, etc.?

- In the I Ching, poles of '1+3' are father-mother resp. heaven-earth plus their 3 daughters and 3 sons. Similarly, Cronos and Rhea had 3 daughters and 3 sons, and their parents Ouranos and Gaia were also heaven (or mountain) and earth.

- If you toss four coins, there is a 50% chance to get '3+1', a 37.5% chance to get '2+2' and only 12.5% to get '4+0'. Even if coins are skew, '3+1' is always more probable than '2+2', and '4+0' only becomes the most probable result once they are about 1:4 skew. Thus, whenever there are 4 things in nature, chances are a priori high that they come as '3+1'.

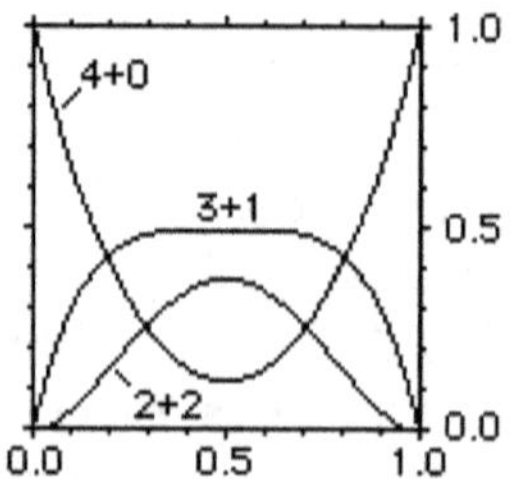

- Time and space come as '1+3'. Their homogeneity implies preservation of energy and momentum. The isotropy of space implies preservation of angular momentum, while time is not invariant to reversal, as entropy never decreases.

  The 4 forces of nature known to date (at everyday energies), electromagnetic, strong, weak and gravitational forces, come as '3+1', since gravitation is the only one closely intertwined with spacetime and without quantum theory.

- In *The Animate and the Inanimate* (1925), William James Sidis observes that inanimate processes can appear alive if time is reversed, using the example of drops of mercury that flow together on a metal surface and then amalgamate with the surface. Reversed in time, drops of mercury would appear to grow out of the metal surface and divide like living cells.

- A trinity is both 3 parts and 1 unit, so 3 turns almost automatically to 3+1, and 4 to 4+1, or a couple+baby, 2+1.

  See also the pythagorean tetractys further below. The image for the universe may have developed from a hill via tetrahedron/pyramid to the dodecahedron in Plato's *Timaeus*, with increasing focus on the number 5 related to Venus, due to the 5 stations of Venus on a 5-pointed star, which is again related to the golden ratio, to harmony, beauty, roundness.

- Before writing, myths were only preserved if people kept remembering and retelling them to younger generations. Thus only stories people really cared about survived. This does, however, not imply that they necessarily consciously understood myths analytically. In a way, myths are sort of informal laws of nature, condense all kinds of experiences into a story. Exploring such unconscious or even intentionally veiled legacy spans ages, is still unfolding, even after Freud and Jung.

  People living in ancient cultures were not wise just from that connotation of 'old'; they were rather young and fresh compared to us who can look back so far into history. But they were also still closer to the 'source' and knew things that got lost or were maybe never explicitly written down. Some things were also truly archaic then, simpler and more brutal; see Homer's Iliad and Odyssey, for example.

- The complex of '1+3' and basic colors is very rich and beautiful, but also a 'can of worms' and only partially fits here, so just some gist below, and see my article "White-red-black and the "green" goddess" under ✺ artemis for more.

- One of the oldest ancient Indian Upanishads, the Chandogya Upanishad (around 700 BCE), speaks of three colors of fire: fire-red, water-white and earth-black.

"The red colour of [gross] fire is the colour of [the original] fire; the white colour of [gross] fire is the colour of [the original] water; the black colour of [gross] fire is the colour of [the original] earth. Thus vanishes from fire what is commonly called fire, the modification being only a name, arising from speech, while the three colours (forms) alone are true." (6.4.1, translated by Swami Nikhilananda)

These three colors, which appear as first colors in apparently all earliest cultures able to write them down, represent most likely a more archaic concept of color as light/fire, as follows.

Without light no colors; fire produces light; so color would be heavily related to light; thus the basic opposites white (bright) and black (dark), plus the color(s) of fire, red-orange-yellow. Water is transparent, earth is often intransparent, ashes are more "fluid" than coal, hence water-white and earth-black.

In ancient Greek, the words for black/white, mélas/leukós, still had, maybe even primarily, the connotation of dark/bright; the word for red, pyrrós, literally says color of fire.

In other words, no fire would have been black, lighting it red, and fire/light would have saturated at white.

- The first 3 of the 4 riders of the apocalypse have the colors white-red-black. The color of the fourth is chlōrós in ancient Greek, thus related to chlorophyll, the substance that makes leaves green. Colorwise, it was most likely a pale green/yellow color, like new shoots of plants or also the color of a corpse.

  In the fairy tale around Baba Yaga, three riders appear, white-day at dawn, red-sun when the sun rises, black-night when it gets dark. They are all explicitly servants of Baba Yaga, who also has three pairs of helping hands, which identify her as the triple moon goddess Hecate-Artemis, who is both a goddess of death and of birth, acting also as midwife in mythology.

  The idea behind this would be that the moon would be the ruling light in the sky because it alone can appear both at day and night, and can even shadow the sun during a total solar eclipse. In folklore, Baby Yaga's house is mobile, stands on chicken legs, the rooster being again a symbol of fire.

- Near the end of Apuleius' *The Golden Ass* (around 150 CE), Apuleius encounters the goddess Isis at full moon at the sea shortly after moonrise:

"Her many-coloured robe was of finest linen; part was glistening white, part crocus-yellow, part glowing red and along the entire hem a woven bordure of flowers and fruit clung swaying in the breeze. But what caught and held my eye more than anything else was the deep black lustre of her mantle. [...] It was embroidered with glittering stars on the hem and everywhere else, and in the middle beamed a full and fiery moon." (Chapter 17, translated by Robert Graves)

Shortly afterwards she describes herself:

"[...] mother of nature, all encompassing mistress of the elements, first progeny of the times, highest power/deity/queen, first/best (sky) deity, uniform face of gods and goddesses, who dispenses over heavenly, shining summits, salty sea breezes [and] the dead down below in earth, which are silently weeped. A single/unique goddess in multiple shapes, with changing rites, many names, worshipped all over the world." (translated by me)

Note that she may be saying that she rules over heaven, sea and earth, as in Zeus, Poseidon and Hades, hence a trinity of air-water-earth, which would make her potentially fire.

Astrologer Antiochus of Athens and physician Galenus of Pergamon attributed colors resp. body fluids (humors) to elements around the time Apuleius lived, based on older roots going back at least partially to Hippocrates: white to water (phlegm, phlegmatic), black to earth (black bile, melancholic), yellow to fire (yellow bile, choleric) and red to air (blood, sanguine), the colors of Isis' dress above, plus stars and moon for the round fifth element in the sky.

This suggests overall that maybe at some point in time air took the place of fire in the fire trinity as in the Chandogya

Upanishad, maybe via breath as a mixture of air and fire, as in pneuma, or maybe Indian Aum (Om), plus maybe water.

"green"	moon	(rules)	"energy"	fire	yellow
white	day	water	liquid	water	white
red	sun	fire	gas	air	red
black	night	earth	solid	earth	black

- In alchemy, also since about at least the time Apuleius lived, the transition of materials toward the philosopher's stone was believed to be black-white-yellow-red, i.e. earth-water-fire-air, which is roughly in order of lightness of the elements and their relatively layered appearance on earth. It is apparently also the order of elements in the four tasks that Venus gives Psyche in *The Golden Ass*. All of this has ancient Egyptian roots, with Osiris, Isis, Horus, Seth, Nephthys, etc., as well as with ancient crafts of creating fake noble metals and gems.

- Fire must have made a great impression on humanity, as it allowed to keep warm and have light at night, to grill, cook and bake food, eventually to bake pottery and to forge metals. It has even been speculated that easier to digest grilled meat allowed humans to grow larger brains. At first presumably people did not know how to make fire themselves, so trees that were known or believed to attract lightning might have been sacred. As lightning comes from the sky, the "fires" in the sky, i.e. sun, moon, planets and stars, would have been identified with deities in the sky that give fire. Hence the main deity would have been in the sky, most likely the moon. The moon can be round like fruits and berries, but also slim and pointy like leaves, and it can grow from the shape of a "catkin" to the round one of a ripe fruit. Attributes of such a deity may thus have been the fruits ripening on such sacred trees in the colors of fire, like mulberries, or similar.

Anything in nature that was not white-red-black would have been unnamed first: green, blue, brown, pale colors like the moon, gleaming colors; often colors that signal something that is not crucial for survival, neither food nor danger. This could explain why green only entered languages late, despite being so predominant in nature. Shapes and colors of fruits may have adapted to preferences of its consumers and they, in turn, their sexually attractive body parts to fruits.

Imagine a child in prehistory in the arms of its mother on a tree at night, trying to "pluck" the moon in the sky, just as it used to pluck fruit and already earlier used to get food from the similarly round breasts of its mother, signaled also by her "red" nipples; thus the gentle, soft roundness of the mother so intimately linked to the moon and the colors of life/fire.

- Elements are elemental necessities of life with air to breathe, water to drink, food to eat, plus energy/warmth, and they are elemental and at times traumatic forces of nature with fires and volcano eruptions, inondations, storms and landslides.

- Robert Graves in the introduction of *The Greek Myths*:

"Ancient Europe had no gods. The Great Goddess was regarded as immortal, changeless, and omnipotent; and the concept of fatherhood had not been introduced into religious thought. She took lovers, but for pleasure, not to provide her children with a father. Men feared, adored, and obeyed the matriarch; the hearth which she tended in a cave or hut being their earliest social centre, and motherhood their prime mystery. Thus the first victim of a Greek public sacrifice was always offered to Hestia of the Hearth. The goddess's white aniconic image, perhaps her most widespread emblem, which appears at Delphi as the *omphalos*, or navel-boss, may originally have represented the raised white mound of tightly-packed ash, enclosing live charcoal, which is the easiest means of preserving fire without smoke."

Again a sequence white-red-black, ash-glow-coal, with almost certainly roots far back into prehistory. The triangle as the mountain on which deities lived, where lightning was more likely to strike, not to speak of volcanoes, or as a pyramid or the symbols for the elements, and so much more.

See also 20.2 and 90.3 in *The Greek Myths* about omphalos, tripods, white-red-black, Crete, the moon-cow Io, and more.

- The fifth element is round like the moon and cyclic motion in the sky; if the first element is fire, then so is the fifth in a circle of elements, thus the moon goddess also a "higher octave" of fire. Of the three goddesses Hera, Athena and Aphrodite, Paris hands the apple to Aphrodite (Venus) because if you cut an apple in half, you get a five-pointed star, like the five stations of Venus over 8 years, where also sun and moon return quite closely to the same positions.

- In the article "Red, White, and Black in Symbolic Thought: The Tricolour Folk Motif, Colour Naming, and Trichromatic Vision" (Folklore, 123:3, 310-329, 2012), Jessica Hemming mentions that red was typically a color that is darker than fresh blood, more towards brown. Now, Menstrual blood can often be darker (already oxidized) than blood from a fresh wound, which would again link to the moon.

  See also her article "Pale horses and green dawns. Elusive colour terms in early Welsh heroic poetry" (North American journal of Celtic studies, Vol 1, No. 2, 189-223, 2017).

- Robert Graves in *The White Goddess* (1948):

  "I write of her as the White Goddess because white is her principal colour, the colour of the first member of her moon-trinity, but when Suidas the Byzantine [ca. 10th century CE] records that Io was a cow that changed her colour from white to rose and then to **black** he means that the New Moon is the white goddess of birth and growth; the Full Moon, the red goddess of love and battle; the Old Moon, the black goddess of death and divination. Suidas's myth is supported by Hyginus's fable [ca. 0 CE] of a heifer-calf born to Minos and Pasiphae which changed its colours thrice daily in the same way. In response to a challenge from an oracle one Polyidus son of Coeranus correctly compared it to a mulberry—a fruit sacred to the Triple Goddess." (Chapter 4)

To me, the colors of the goddess would not directly reflect the change of visible colors of the moon during its phases, as one might think at first, but rather represent the hidden powers that make it change, which would confirm Graves above:

The white goddess would be the power that makes the new moon brighter (more "white") again, towards full moon, from little baby girl to maiden, growth. The red goddess would be the fertile adult woman, who menstruates (red blood); she would make the moon pregnant, the round "belly" of the full moon. The **black** goddess would make the moon darker (more "black") again, towards new moon, withering towards crone. The "red phase" would be somewhat abstract as the blood would only come to light at menstruation if the bearer did not get pregnant. I guess the idea would have been that the child's blood and body would have grown from that.

So the seed for a new child would be expected to grow each month from sometime after new moon until ovulation around full moon and, if the bearer did not get pregnant, would result in menstrual bleeding around new moon. Note, however, that most contemporary women do not have their individual cycles correlated with moon phases. The average cycle is 28 days (but varies quite a bit individually), which is closer to the time it takes the moon to return to the same spot relative to the fixed stars (27.3 days) than to new moon (29.5 days).

- Empedocles would have been the first to speak of four elements, according to Aristotle in *Metaphysics* (Book I 3) and in *On Generation and Corruption* (Book I 1).

Since at least then, Empedocles is usually credited for having first mentioned the four elements, in the following fragment (DK31B6) of a poem usually called *On Nature*:

> τέσσαρα γὰρ πάντων ῥιζώματα πρῶτον ἄκουε·
> Ζεὺς ἀργὴς Ἥρη τε φερέσβιος ἠδ' Ἀιδωνεύς
> Νῆστίς θ', ἣ δακρύοις τέγγει κρούνωμα βρότειον.

It speaks of "fourtold roots" at the origin of all, and then lists four deities with some attributes, in this order: Zeus (flashing/shining), Hera (live-giving/-bearing), Aidoneus (no attributes), Nestis (moisture, tears/dew).

Interpreting the deities as *roots* of the elements, Zeus with his thunderbolt would be fire, pregnant Hera earth, Hades, who's name means "unseen", air, and Nestis obviously water.

The quote is from a work by Aetius (1st or 2nd century CE), which has only indirectly survived in several later works attributed to different authors. Mostly elements are attributed the same way as me above, else earth and air are flipped.

It is obviously tempting to interpret Zeus as white, pregnant Hera as **red** and Hades as **black**, in the ancient order of a ripening mulberry, plus Nestis as great goddess, especially since Nestis might be the the same goddess as the Egyptian Nephthys, who Robert Graves calls "the Egyptian Hecate" in *The White Goddess* (in the chapter *Gwion's Heresy*).

- In ancient Egypt, Osiris stood for **black**, the fertile earth of the Nile valley; his brother Seth for **red**, the desert East and West of the valley. The mythological killing and dismembering of Osiris by Seth presumably reflects that in prehistoric times sometime after the annual flood the soil would dry up and become fractured into a mosaic of slabs, or even into sand and dust. Fortunately, every year the Nile, white Isis (also like milk), would restore Osiris to life with water and the fresh fertile black sediments carried along.

  This is certainly an oversimplification of Egyptian mythologies that evolved over millennia, but likely still captures a core.

- See this absolutely stunning article by the Ethiopian "Shakespeare", Tsegaye Gabre-Medhin: *The Origin of the Trinity in Art & Religion: Ethiopian Roots in the Egypto-Greek & Hebrew*, on page 99-120 of *African Origins of the Major World Religions*, ed. Amon Saba Saakana, Karnak House, 1988.

  KaBaRa to Kabbalah and Kaaba, Egypt as Kamit (black land), sacred tree, Osiris to Moses and others, and so much more. I guess Fela's song *Shakara* might fit in, too.

- First Corinthians 13:13: "And now these three remain: faith, hope, and love. But the greatest of these is love." The Greek words are pístis, elpís and agápē, which are also goddesses, and they occur prominently in Plato's philosophy.

Faith could be interpreted as sun, bright/white, Hera; hope as moon, dark/black, Athena; love as Venus, fire/red, Aphrodite, the one that got the apple from Paris. These planets are also the order of dresses in the 19th century fairy tale *Three nuts for Cinderella* by Božena Němcová: sun, moon, stars, which reminds also of Isis' dress. Actually, these three occur already in Mesopotamia in the 12th century BC on a stele: Venus for Ishtar, moon and sun for the gods Sin and Shamash.

- A closer look at the passage from the Chandogya Upanishad mentioned further above shows that the word used for red, *rohitam*, is also the word for a female red deer, as well as as Rohini the name of the red star Aldebaran, one of the eyes of the bull in the constellation Taurus. In ancient Greece deer were sacred to the moon goddess Artemis, originally probably because antlers resemble a fire. In ancient Egypt in the first dynasties the Pharaoh used to run with the white-**red**-**black** Apis bull at the beginning of spring when the constellation of Taurus was rising. The moon goddess resides at birth and death, as both midwife and goddess of death, when the new or old moon look like a flame or a shoot, or later in history a bow or a sickle, hence she is also celebrated at the beginning of spring when nature starts to sprout again.

The first version of *The White Goddess*, which Robert Graves wrote after new moon in the third degree of Taurus in spring

1944, was titled *The Roebuck in the Thicket*. Isis as the only woman in Isis-Seth-Osiris would be white, hence *The White Goddess* a fitting settled title? Hail Artemis!

Note that in astrology the moon is exalted (a good guest) in the 3rd degree of Taurus, or maybe around 3° (see Vettius Valens, *Anthology*, book 3, chapter 4, 2nd century CE).

- Note that way more could be said around these themes; for example, water-white is also closely related to milk and the "mound" it comes from, or cows and the milky way and Isis as the Nile; the three Graeae (grey women) and their single eye, the three Fates and their fabric; purple Io like mulberry juice and the famous die, as well as drinking wine from amethyst goblets in Greek antiquity; the three Indian gunas (strands, chords) in the colors white, red and black, as well as the four varnas (colors) of social classes, with additionally yellow, all maybe related to ancient Egyptian Ma'at; Ra as a yellow cat with donkey ears defeating the white-red-black Apophis snake wrapped around a green tree with red fruits in a painting in Theban Tomb 359 of the 20th dynasty (12th century BCE); as just a few of millions of examples. . .

Note that it were possibly similar depictions of Ra that led to medieval depictions of "killer rabbits" after the crusades.

- A link from elements to fire is immediately easier to trace than one to the moon, which may be because this would have been a secret, the unspeakable real name of the goddess?

- Plato talks about colors in the *Timaeus*, Aristotle in *On Sense and the Sensible*. Both start with black and white as basic colors, which is scientifically correct in the sense that by selectively taking frequencies out of the full spectrum of white, you get all colors, including black and white.

  There are three kinds of color sensors in the human eye, for red, green and blue, sorted from low to high frequency. None triggered (no light) is black, plus red gives red, plus also green gives yellow, plus also blue gives white, hence a sequence black-red-yellow-white or earth-air-fire-water.

  In Plato's *Critias* the stones of Atlantis' architecture are won locally and have the colors white, black and red.

- Is attribution of colors and animals to points of the compass in the Lakota "Medicine Wheel" relatively new, dating to some time after the arrival of Europeans in America, or did it maybe already come to America with immigrants walking across the Bering Sea maybe over 10'000 years ago ?

  The four points of the compass, plus a center, would be one reason for 4+1 elements.

- The Yangshao culture "Xishuipo M45 Tomb" in China, which dates back to the 4th millennium BCE, features the mosaic of a tiger opposite the mosaic of a dragon, as constellations in the sky, exactly the animals that are traditionally assigned to West and East in China. Ra's nightly fight with the Apep/Apophis snake reminds of the phoenix and snake (plus turtle) standing for South and North in China.

- Aristotle considers four "causes" in *Physics* and *Metaphysics*, which remind of the four elements. Matter reminds of earth, form of air, primary source of fire and final goal of water.

- Some fragments of Heraclitus might suggest the same circle as Aristotle. DK22B76 seems to mention all four elements in the same circle, earth-fire-air-water-earth, but the original text cannot be restored for sure, according to Diels/Kranz (DK) in *Die Fragmente der Vorsokratiker*. See also fragments

B31 and B36; and B90 might suggest that Heraclitus would have considered fire the primary substance.

- See the pythagorean tetractys and oath. Pythagoras lived in the 6th century BCE, before Empedocles and Hippocrates. The tetractys is a triangle with four dots on each side:

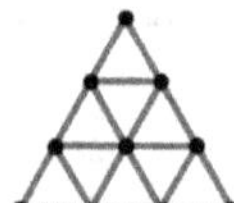

1	point	monad (unity)
2	line	dyad (power)
3	triangle/plane	triad (harmony)
4	tetrahedron/space	tetrad (cosmos)

It relates also to music via the ratios between each line, octave (2:1), perfect fifth (3:2) and perfect fourth (4:3).

The list reminds of fire-air-water-earth (light to heavy).

But the above is apparently even more than usually for early Greek philosophers based on speculation, since Pythagoras reportedly never wrote anything down himself, so that there are even less credible sources about his views in his time, often surrounded by legends bordering on religion/sect.

DK note that practically the same word that Empedocles used for "roots" in DK31B6 also appears in the pythagorean oath in DK58B15, with both fragments dating back to Aetius in early CE, so once more circular paths.

- To ancient Greeks, the ancient Egyptians were apparently sort of like the ancient Greeks in modern perception, an admired ancient culture. It appears that the ancient Egyptians might have kept things more secret than the Greeks in their time, maybe only passing it on from master to pupil adept?

- As a playful teaser, note that the pyramids have five corners, an earthly base of four, plus one on top...

With maybe even opposites attached as below (or maybe with dry/hot and wet/cold flipped, or attached to faces instead), reflecting the heating and drying effect of the sun during the course of a day, similarly to the original image for yin-yang in China as the shady and sunny sides of a hill?

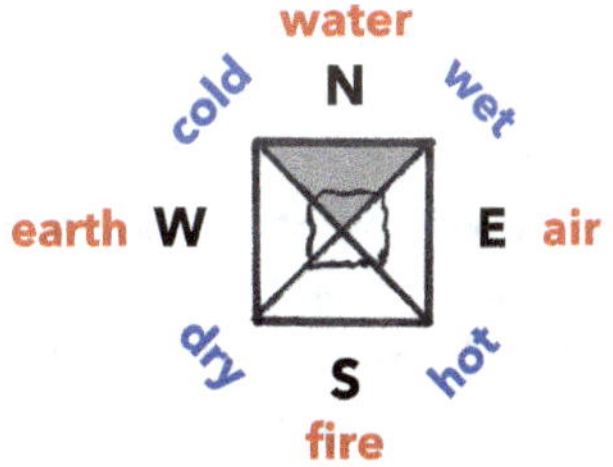

But how pyramids evolved from single "floor" mastabas via step pyramids to their final form seems to be well researched. Especially how Sneferu had the first three pyramids without steps built and the first two attempts failed, does not suggest that all that much elemental symbolism would have been in the conscious minds of ancient Egyptians at that time.

- Antiochus of Athens attributed elements to seasons the same way I did with faces of the pyramids, if winter is north, etc.: spring-air, summer-fire, autumn-earth and winter-water. The symbols for the four elements are triangles, reminding of the four faces of a pyramid, so whoever created those symbols might maybe have related elements to pyramids.

The symbols also stand for female and male sexes, overlaid to a hexagram "as above so below" for intercourse between Gaia (earth) and Ouranos (sky). △ ◬ ▽ ▿ → ✡

- In the *Timaeus* Plato does not stop at the platonic solids for the elements, but explicitly constructs all of them except the dodecahedron ('fifth element') from right-angled triangles, actually even as '1+3' with '1' being the cube (earth).

- Zeus, Poseidon and Hades ruled in heaven (air), sea (water) and underworld (earth). Life can exist in all three of these elements, but not in fire, except in legend fire salamanders.

- In August 2015, I assigned Greek goddesses to pairs of elements and moon phases, and tentatively flipped Athena and Hera in May 2018: Artemis/Hecate to birth/death at new moon as fire around water, Hera (and Clotho) to growth as a young woman or girl at the first quarter as earth around air, Aphrodite (and Lachesis) to bloom as a mature woman at full moon as water around fire, and Athena (and Atropos) to withering as an old woman at the last quarter as air around earth. Artemis/Hecate would thus contain both first and fifth element, and elements would touch as on the Möbius Strip.

- Zhuangzi's famous butterfly dream:

"Once Chuang Tzu dreamt that he was a butterfly, a fluttering butterfly who felt at ease and happy and knew nothing of Chuang Tzu. Suddenly he woke up: Then he was again really and truly Chuang Tzu. Now I do not know whether Chuang Tzu dreamt that he was a butterfly or whether the butterfly dreamt that it was Chuang Tzu, even though there is certainly a difference between Chuang Tzu and the butterfly. This is how the change of things is." (translated by me from the Wilhelm translation to German)

The same day I had first quoted the dream here, on the streets of Zürich, two butterflies on a truck, 21 Sep 2016 at 13:34. White, red, black, a little yellow, even a little circle and her.

(In Apuleius' encounter with Isis, it is left open whether he was "just dreaming" or "it really happened".)

The image is by Elena Vizerskaya (Getty Images 108350631); I bought the rights to use it, too, just to be safe.

- (The walking cat of the *metamorphosis* section came to me at Delphi in Greece on Tuesday, 4 September 2018 at about 13:09, ate some of my food, a dry pretzel and salmon jerky, then, after a few burps (still a kid) and playing a little, took a nap of about 20 minutes on my lap, then left roughly in the direction of the Athena Pronoia temple, where I had been a bit earlier. During these few minutes there were no doubts what to do and felt so good, like having a child to care for. Was the AC maybe even an oracle for the AC of π, with the moon maybe late at glowing quincunxes, or early spring with almost shared progressed moons? Late, beyond doubt.)

evolutions

Some ways in which the idea presented earlier might evolve with time...

mixed feelings

The inner elements eri and emi are softer than the outer ones, which suggests that they would *mix* more easily.

The idea is now that what appears outside as individual and separate beings is unconsciously connected inside...

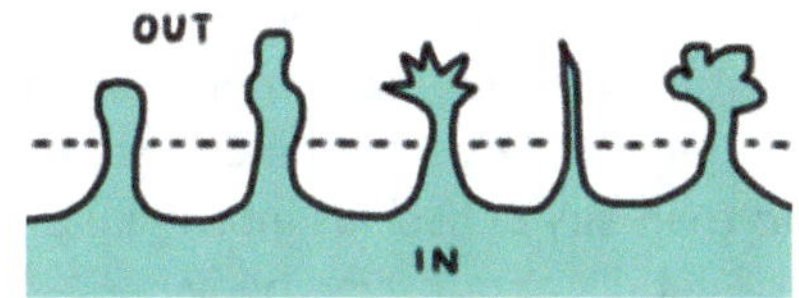

...and that these connections result in feelings that change for often not obvious reasons (emi), while naming inner concepts allows to impose some abstract calm (eri).

Astrology links water (emi) to feelings, love, music, art, religion, the collective and/or individual unconscious, and more. Now, the idea of a *collective* unconscious goes back to Jung, while it may in the end still be so that such unconscious collective connections are created by more Freudian individual unconsciouses, via subliminal channels in normal day-to-day external interactions between beings.

But let me explore things in the Jungian picture first, as a Gedankenexperiment, because it is initially easier, and because it mirrors the initial assumption more directly.

How one feels at any moment would be a mixture of individual and collective influences. Not that what other people think would be directly accessible, just indirectly with regard to how one feels in a particular situation, or how one feels regarding individual possible next steps.

Individuals that are emotionally and physically close would likely have the strongest influence on a person, but also large groups of people, like same village, country, religion, etc., could together have a strong influence.

Influences from a collective unconscious could go well beyond the sum of what is in individual conscious minds. Since the collective unconscious would effectively be a very large brain, consisting of many more brain cells than any individual being, it might have a much more complex and sophisticated mind than any conscious individual and it could know all kinds of details about everybody.

Such a view of a collective unconscious would resemble the concept of god or gods in many religions, and it would likely be fragmented into smaller units at several scales, like families, countries, religions, etc., each with its own collective feelings, plans, and so on.

Jung noticed that in dreams and in cultural creations some archetypal patterns repeat. These archetypes might simply be part of the thoughts, experiences and knowledge of the collective unconscious.

Precognition in dreams or art might simply be picking up collective intentions that are only later realized and can be felt and dreamed about already while the collective unconscious is only planning or considering them.

How would the collective unconscious effectively direct the individuals it consists of? Telling each and every one what to do at each moment would likely not be possible, just like the conscious individual mind would not be able to tell each of its nerve cells when to fire.

But maybe with a general concept like astrology, which creates a balanced and relatively complete set of individuals, each with its own approach to new problems? Faced with a particular problem, a Leo, for example, would feel more like solving it in a "Leo way", due to collective feedback, so that in any situation different approaches would be tried by different individuals and a good solution would usually emerge. Since astrology tries to reflect all possible approaches in a structured way, the search space for solutions would usually be quite complete.

In other words, a culture with a system like astrology would have an evolutionary advantage in the sense of Darwin. Astrology would then not necessarily need to have anything to do with planets and stars in the sky, more so with relatively ancient beliefs about them.

Assuming the collective unconscious would extend to matter considered inanimate, oracles like the I Ching or Tarot could really reveal some intentions of the collective unconscious, maybe paired with emotional feedback which parts of the response to focus on or how to interpret it. If so, also astrology might a priori still have natural causes, direct influences from planets and stars, collective feedback from the universe itself.

However, there are some arguments that speak against astrology having dominantly natural causes from the sky. There are different astrologies in different cultures, each of which comes in different flavours and has different schools of thought. Besides many small examples for a detachment from actual constellations in the sky, the most prominent one is Pluto in Western astrology.

Pluto was at its discovery in 1930 thought to be a planet that is about as big as planet Earth. Over the following decades it first emerged that Pluto is much smaller, consists mainly of ice and finally in the early 21st century that Pluto is rather part of a belt of objects in similar orbits and with similar sizes. In 20th century astrology, however, Pluto was attributed a major role, both in mundane events and personal fates. In my perception, part of that view *did* reflect reality, so that it seems most plausible to me that astrology is *largely* a cultural creation of mankind that works by collective feedback.

Now let me come back to the initial question or to how something with the properties of a collective unconscious could come about in view of contemporary physics.

The most immediate explanation would be that there are direct connection between brains, mediated by some kind of "waves". But this can largely be excluded today, except maybe at close range, in the sense that any explanation of that sort would require new physics.

So let me focus on known physics and try to look for the most simple and obvious explanation. What I propose is that people simply *mirror* who and what they encounter in their lives inside their brains.

People's brains would thus contain "copies" of everyone they know, most prominently and precisely of their loved ones. What exactly the neural networks would mirror would not be consciously available to individuals nor would it likely be easy to analyze scientifically even if the full structure was known. But it could in principle allow people to make fairly accurate predictions about what their loved ones would do and when. For example, one person could possibly think of the other one almost exactly the moment that other person would have picked up the phone to call.

In terms of network terminology, this would be a *store and forward* network instead of one where information is propagated immediately.

leads

- Mirroring the outside world is such a central part of the human psyche that it would seem likely that nature would try to make use of any physical effect it could.

- Experimentally distinguishing different effects that could explain such phenomena seems to be very difficult.

- Candidates would include entangled quantum states, as in the EPR paradox, and self-similarity as in fractals.

  There would be neither senders nor receivers in these views; sharing would be fundamentally symmetric. Would maybe different people simply look at the *same* things inside?

  If there was just one inner world, seen from different perspectives by different people, similarly to what is usually assumed about the outer world, would maybe the inner world be as important or "real" as the outer one, or even more, unlike nowadays usually assumed in science and technology?

- See "Zeitzeugnisse" under ☞ artemis for earlier contributions by me to some possibly new physics related to this, which make additional very specific predictions, and also "How astrology might really work?" for a more recent and longer article around the same themes as here, but with different starting point and focus, also available in German.

- Big data and deep learning could be used to find and analyze such collective structures, including astrological ones.

- Science is based on some implicit, but fundamentally unprovable assumptions, like that nature is more stupid than people and repeats stoically given the same questions. Since numbers only come to be after a measurement, it is difficult to compare a mathematical model of the situation before measurement with reality. So, the "Veil of Isis" may not be easy to lift, if at all, also related to e5, etc.

star signs

Star signs in the Western zodiac seem to reflect transitions between elements within Aristotle's circle.

Fire signs seem to transform from earth via fire to air, while water is missing, thus desired:

The archetypal image is simply a fire that transforms wood (earth) to smoke (air). Aries as a young fire has most earth, Leo most fire, Sagittarius most air.

In psychological astrology a wound is a central theme for the two later fire signs Leo and Sagittarius, namely for the fisher king in Perceval and Chiron in mythology.

In the model that wound is simply the human body (earth) that is wounded by the fire of life, as any human body must die one day. Only what is learned in life can be formulated in words (air) and can thus be passed on to later generations, thus becomes immortal in a way. So there is a transformation from mortal body to immortal mind, or from animal via man/king to god.

Learning and getting compassion—the element water that is missing in the transformation of the fire signs—in the process is a vital goal for older fire signs.

Air signs seem to transform from fire via air to water, while earth is missing, thus desired:

The archetypal image is a cloud (air), which emits both lightning (fire) and rain (water). Gemini as young air has most fire, Libra most air, Aquarius most water.

Paris, who is associated with Libra, chose Aphrodite's offering of love and marriage with Helena, the most beautiful woman in the world, hence love (water) and thus the possibility for the missing element earth in the form of children as fruits of love. Similarly, the opening of Pandora's Box, associated with Aquarius, symbolizes birth.

Water signs seem to transform from earth via water to air, while fire is missing, thus desired:

The archetypal image is a river with Cancer as a source and young river emerging from the mountains, maybe from a glacier (earth), merging with more and more rivers and becoming a stream as Scorpio (water) and finally flowing into the sea as Pisces from where most water eventually evaporates again (air), by the power of the sun (fire), the missing element and goal for the water signs.

So, the transition is, like for the fire signs, from earth to air, but this time for a passive, female element. The river that flows down to the sea is more fated than fire, since it is passive, it cannot resist the movement.

But the way up in the end towards light is important, like, for example, for the crab that bit Heracles into his ankle while he was fighting the Hydra in the swamps, and got its place in the sky as the constellation Cancer.

Earth signs seem to transform from fire via earth to water, while air is missing, thus desired:

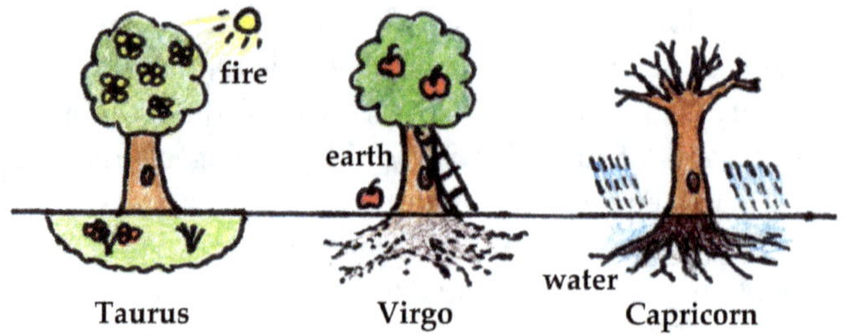

The archetypal image is a tree with Taurus focussing on the directly visible, but short-lived beauties of the tree that grow with the power of the sun (fire), Capricorn restraining himself to the parts of the tree that persist across seasons and which keep it from falling down, namely trunk and roots, which feed it with water and the substances diluted in it, and Virgo in between, between beauty and fate.

It is this fate or necessity, which creates minimal structures like the branches and roots of a tree, thus order, the abstract element air.

This solves the riddle that even though Virgo is often depicted as being very concerned about order, many Virgos

do not keep their lives and homes in strict order. It is Virgo
for whom order is an *issue*, for Capricorn it is a *given* and
for Taurus it is not that important, except a bit, as Taurus
is transforming from fire to earth.

Persephone, who is associated with Virgo, was collect-
ing flowers as a maiden, looking at the sunny (fire) side
of life, but already starting to look down to earth, starting
to wonder about how things work, what makes the flowers
grow, etc., when the earth opened up, Hades abducted her
and she became his wife, the queen of the underworld.

For all elements transitions start with a dry element and
end with a wet one. This mirrors that often when one gets
older, one realizes that things are not so clearly and reliably
what they appeared to be when first encountered.

element	transition	desired	image
fire	earth $\rightarrow$ fire $\rightarrow$ air	water	fire
air	fire $\rightarrow$ air $\rightarrow$ water	earth	cloud
water	earth $\rightarrow$ water $\rightarrow$ air	fire	river
earth	fire $\rightarrow$ earth $\rightarrow$ water	air	tree

How about trying to synthesize the properties of the
star signs formally from the transition between the elements
defined by in/out and rest/move alone, without relying on
properties of actual fire, air, water and earth?

ero $\rightarrow$ **emo** $\rightarrow$ eri $(\rightarrow$ emi$)$
emo $\rightarrow$ **eri** $\rightarrow$ emi $(\rightarrow$ ero$)$
ero $\rightarrow$ **emi** $\rightarrow$ eri $(\rightarrow$ emo$)$
emo $\rightarrow$ **ero** $\rightarrow$ emi $(\rightarrow$ eri$)$

Libra, for example, learns from observation of motion
outside (fire) and inside (water). Since Libra's transition is
towards water, the gift of "inner vision" is given to Teiresias

by Zeus and outer vision is reduced by Hera, except for observing omens, which are arguably just outer reflections of collective inner intentions. The transformation would not be exclusively in the direction shown above, rather there would be some back and forth, but summed up, it would be; it would essentially lead inward for all star signs.

For earth signs, the transition would be to channel motion outside into a fixed "vessel" and then to let it flow again inside, desiring to learn something about nature. For air signs, the transition would be to observe outside, learn its laws inside and thus also to derive how things flow inside, desiring to change outer reality for the better. For water signs, the transition would be to let impressions of the outer state flow inside and learn from them, desiring to get things outside moving. For fire signs, the transition would be to get things outside moving and then learning inside how they work, desiring to feel the inner flow.

As another example, the abduction of Kore into the underworld as Persephone is her way into inner worlds, where Hades is more deeply immersed, as Scorpio is already more inside than Virgo, while both are still connected to outside: Hades at least went out to abduct her; she in the end only spends part of the year inside, down in the underworld.

Of course, this was just a partial sketchy first view.

leads

- For more detailed expositions, see the longer article *Elementary star signs* under ⌐ artemis or my book *Elementary Star Signs*, which are both also available in German.
- The four tasks of Psyche in Apuleius' *The Golden Ass* seem to mirror the same transitions very beautifully and precisely, in the order earth-water-fire-air, with goals air-fire-water-earth.
- Are there similar elemental transitions in the Chinese zodiac?

artemis

The oddest thing of all, the thing that most strikes us when we embark on a story is the total void spreading out before us. The events have occurred and lie all around us in a continuous, formless mass without beginning or end. We can start anywhere... — Věra Linhartová

avantgarde

Welcome

- Welcome to my garden...
- Bienvenue dans mon jardin...
- Willkommen in meinem Garten...
- What is exactphilosophy?

I Ching

- Elemental changes in the I Ching?
- Elementare Wandlungen im I Ging?

Astrology

- Elementary star signs
- Elementare Sternzeichen
- Deep Learning and astrology
- Deep Learning und Astrologie

First mention of Lilith
as second focal point of the lunar orbit
Erste Erwähnung von Lilith
als zweitem Brennpunkt der Mondbahn

Dada und Duchamps Fountain
Dada and Duchamp's Fountain
Dada et la Fontaine de Duchamp

Original ideas in the book "Elementary Star Signs"
Eigene Ideen im Buch "Elementare Sternzeichen"

Myths

White-red-black and triple moon goddess?
White-red-black and the "green" goddess

Public Relations

Teslacard Postcard Action 2010
Teslacard Postkarten-Aktion 2010

Mountain Astrologer ads
Mountain Astrologer Anzeigen

Delphi for Palm OS
Delphi für Palm OS

Helicopters in the Renaissance
Hélicoptères à la Renaissance
Helikopter in der Renaissance

In your dreams
In deinen Träumen

Books I never wrote

Metapoliteia

Direct-democratic-federalistic-sustainable world
Direktdemokratisch-föderalistisch-nachhaltige Welt

Zeitzeugnisse

- Discoveries revisited
- Web archives
- First mentions
- odyssey in usenet
- Mondfaden
- Möbius lego
- Timeline

Art

- Die neugierige Statue
- En attendant... / Waiting for... / Warten auf Todog
- Elemental improvisation
- Babysteps 2019 2020
- Visual art gallery

synthesis

Eventually synthesize something tangible from elements defined in terms of in/out, rest/move, and their transformations; hopefully including new physics. . .

measurement

Using a camera, emo and ero could be defined as the difference between two images taken shortly after each other. Differing pixels would be emo, same pixels ero. For example, a ball that rolls down a slope would itself not be emo as a physical object, but emo would be the area the ball spawns between the two images (excluding the middle if the ball is uniformly colored).

A camera can only register ero and emo, and thus only transitions ero ↔ emo, while transitions that would cross between in and out would not be part of the picture.

Measurement inside might be done indirectly by measuring brain activity, or maybe by considering what is recurring inside, some maybe rather abstract insights (eri).

The most basic form of eri might be pairs of opposites, which could maybe be assembled to form more complex concepts, possibly inspired or guided by zodiacs and similar cultural concepts.

leads

- Even if a formal model of the elements defined in terms of in/out and rest/move and their transformations grew into a 'scientific way of doing metaphysics', as aimed at in Kant's *Prolegomena to Any Future Metaphysics That Will Be Able to Present Itself as a Science*, it would essentially be air, something that rests inside the mind (eri). It would not be complete without also including the other three elements in some form, say, in performance art, or whatever.

- Moreover, it would likely not be possible to deduce the whole world from the definition of elements alone, at least doing so would likely be as hard as finding a theory of everything in modern science. Some additional, a priori unprovable assumptions would be necessary to synthesize the world.

- The concept of a "ball" is a priori much more complex than comparing two images, which becomes evident once you try to program computers to recognize (3-dimensional) items on 2-dimensional images. How a ball comes to be in the mind appears to require a lot of interaction with the environment (often quite early as a child), and in the end it is philosophically not so clear whether a "ball" is rather a natural thing, something that objectively exists, or instead rather a purely abstract cultural creation useful for interaction with others. See also Kant or Plato's Allegory of the Cave.

  The above definition of emo $\leftrightarrow$ ero appears thus fundamental, but is possibly already different from immediate experience of the world in which a rolling ball is never seen as two crescents. It reminds also of the shadows in Plato's Cave, which even remind of the souls of the dead that dwell in Hades as shadows, as depicted in Homer's Odyssey. In other words, the above definition might already project reality onto something in which crucial information might already be lost, or not.

- Could maybe only activity cross between in and out, but not elements? Would activity travelling from in to out transform both eri to emi and ero to emo? That would at least be consistent with a camera only recording ero and emo.

- In a harmonic oscillator, two kinds of energies are transformed into each other. For example, for a mass on a spring, the energy in the spring transforms into the kinetic energy of the moving mass and vice-versa. This gives the motion of the oscillator four special states, when either of the energies is extremal. And the motion between these states is periodic, thus overall reminding of the circle of elements.

However, the natural pairing of extremal states of a harmonic oscillator is opposite states in the cycle, which naturally fits rest/move in the elemental circle, but makes it hard to relate two pairs of *adjacent* states to opposites like active/passive or in/out in a natural way.

- The four elements can be grouped into 3 different pairs with opposing attributes, including maybe these:

rest/move	in/out	passive/active
bind/release	wet/dry	cold/hot
	soft/hard	heavy/light
	malleable/brittle	inert/swift
	mixed/isolated	dense/thin
	collective/individual	dark/light
		female/male
		moon/sun
		night/day
		un-/conscious

Some pairs on the right have a historically patriarchal touch, which however still partially reflects nature.

psyche

Given the immediate experience of life would be essentially along the circle of elements, everything the psyche does and experiences, like thinking and feeling, would also essentially be along that circle. In other words, life as personal experience (psyche) would essentially happen along that circle.

In the model of elemental transformations in the zodiac from the *star signs* section, all star signs transform from outer to inner elements (except for the desired element). Inside is where one might suspect the psyche to be.

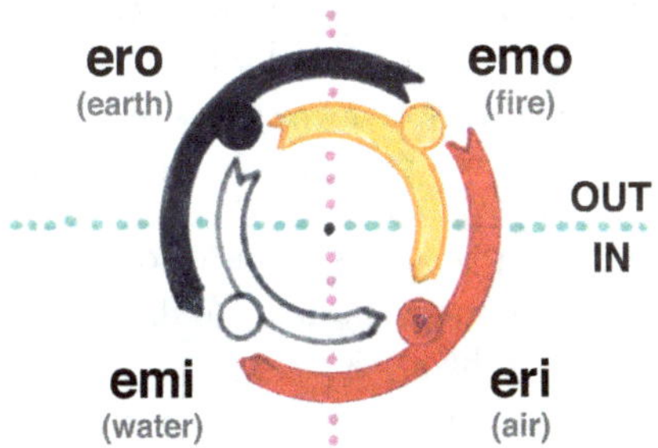

Could the argument be reversed, would an assumption that the psyche is inside imply the transitions of the zodiac ? At least they are general in the sense that for each element they select the transition from the outer adjacent element via the element itself to the inner adjacent element.

So all transformations in life would be about learning in the broadest sense, end up inside, but with hopes also for outside, maybe even often as offspring, new life.

And the psyche would be closely related to e5.

leads

- The four tasks of Psyche in Apuleius' *The Golden Ass* are about elemental transformations of nominally the *psyche*.

  The four tasks are in the middle of the book, nested threefold into the outer story of Lucius as an ass, the fairy tale of Cupid and Psyche, and Psyche's visits to different deities for help, until she ends up at Venus who poses the four tasks to her.

  While the two outmost stories are based in part on well-known older myths and folk tales, and the ancient gods reflect their well-known natures, this appears not to be the case for Psyche's tasks. Instead it is more likely that Apuleius devised them himself or at least that they emerged around his time, as a way to convey certain new ideas.

  Only few of Apuleius' works have survived. One is *On Plato and his Doctrine*, a biography of Plato plus an outline of part of Plato's philosophy, another one is *On the God of Socrates*. He also translated Plato's *Phaedo* from Greek to Latin, where Socrates argues for the immortality of the soul on the evening before his death by hemlock.

  The word that Plato used for soul is *psychê*, literally ancient Greek for a *butterfly*, that mystical short-lived creature.

A butterfly is often seen as either resting on a flower or else fluttering on to the next one, which reminds of the psyche, which often dwells a while on a topic, then "flutters" on to the next, often also in a rather random looking way.

Apuleius lived in a very fruitful time in which many symbolic systems found a form to stay in for many centuries by melting Greek and Egyptian/African views into something new: Star signs got their attributed elements; in Stoicism the highest, lightest form of pneuma was called psychê; in alchemy the transition towards the philosopher's stone black-white-yellow-red is the same order of elements as apparently in Psyche's tasks; a mummy reminds of the chrysalis into which a caterpillar weaves itself and later emerges as a butterfly, a cocoon as sort of a vessel towards a higher life; leading back in time to silkworms, the changing colors of a mulberry and the great goddess, or forward to then upcoming religions like Christianity that feature the idea of an immortal soul, and so on.

The original title of the book was *Metamorphoseon Libri XI*, which is likely why Apuleius might have devised the tasks of Psyche as elemental transformations of the soul and placed them at the very center of his masterpiece.

- Myths may have carved out the cycle of elements more closely and in a more streamlined way than most other stories, as in myths originally only what felt ultimately important was worth the effort of remembering it by heart during life and transmitting it orally from one generation to the next. Myths around star signs, in particular, might even more specifically reflect only certain segments of the cycle of elements.

- Observing something that happens outside (emo) can lead to insights into the workings of the world (eri), so the psyche would have operated along the circle of elements, emo → eri. Natural sciences would be a lot about this part of the cycle, relating essentially experiment (emo) and theory (eri).

  You could, for example, not learn much of what a cube is, unless it moves (emo) or if you move yourself and look at it from various angles or turn it in your hand (eri → emo). Just looking at a cube from a single perspective (ero) would not allow to learn much about a cube as a physical object with specific properties and symmetries, but could still change your mood (emi). Such a mood might still allow to learn something in the sense of later being able to recognize a cube if you encounter another one from a similar angle, but not much in a consciously analytical way, and arguably recognition might rather come indirectly from a transition emi → eri, from learning inside from different moods.

Even though in the model of the star signs, transitions would in the end tend to go inside, in practice things would often involve both ways, for example, when looking at a cube from different sides, both moving it, eri → emo, and learning from its movements, emo → eri, in a close feedback loop.

At emi much more may already be going on unconsciously than is obvious, there may already be a lot of comparing of different experiences (ero) happening in the background, which then eri could analyze by observing emi inside similarly to emo outside. And what eri would postulate, would again create an emotional reaction, and so on, to be ruminated.

- How would the maybe more subtle view of dual female and male elements in the I Ching fit here? And generally into the astrological model of transformations in the Western zodiac? What about the Chinese zodiac, which probably emerged roughly around the year zero like similar systems in the West? Does it also mirror elemental transitions of the psyche? Or maybe something else? What about other zodiacs?

- Is it true that the psyche is inside, that all would travel inside during life, or is that more of a Western view, not ultimately true? But maybe part of the truth if adding similar transitions "the other way" to balance it, or in some other ways?

- In prehistory the psyche may not have been much able, yet, to distinguish what it can influence outside vs. inside: The world of the psyche would have first consisted only of the state outside, ero (dark/black/earth), the flow inside, emi (light/white/water), plus life, eri and emo (fire/red). Hence what could be thought inside and done outside would have been mixed into a single experience of daily life, while the outer state of the world and the inner flow of feelings seemed essentially given, predominantly beyond human control.

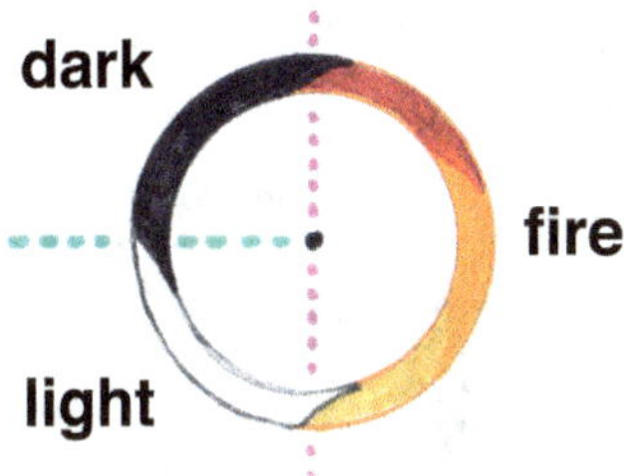

- Colors do not fit perfectly in the prehistoric circle. Black fits well with earth and white fits well with water, but ero, as it is outside, would at first seem brighter than emi which is inside.

  But maybe this is again thinking too much in today's terms: The outside world might only seem bright due to light (fire) like from the sun, but in itself would be dark, as revealed at night. Similarly, inside the mind is not like inside a dark cave, but can be arbitrarily filled with light at day and night.

  Of course, the ability to first preserve and later on create fire would have made a great difference in those respects.

  Note that I switched the fire colors in the illustration so that the darker color (red) is closer to black and the lighter color (yellow) closer to white, actually as in alchemy.

- Before agriculture, people essentially had to follow nature. Where to stay, where to find something to eat, was beyond human control. Similarly, the flow of feelings, dreams, visions was not something people could approach analytically at first. That probably came in time by telling stories, with mythology and other stories. Abstract concepts like love were first personified as deities like Aphrodite/Venus, only later things became more abstract, as in Greek philosophy.

- Reading a text silently was apparently not usually done in antiquity. Texts were rather recited aloud, hence also texts often in rhymes to give them rhythm and melody. Thus in and out of what the psyche actively did were still somewhat mixed up into one: no thinking without speaking or acting.

- The circle reminds of the Lakota "Medicine Wheel", as well as of other similar circles, including the Chinese one.

Akta Lakota Museum (aktalakota.stjo.org)

References

- Andreas Schöter. *Bipolar Change*. Journal of Chinese Philosophy. Volume 35, Issue 2, p. 297-317 (June 2008).

  Abstract I reconsider the natural characterization of change and non-change that arises from the algebraic approach: this sees change as yang in contrast to nonchange, which is yin. Following a persuasive example from Alain Stalder, rather than consider change solely in contrast to non-change, I develop a formal characterization of different forms of change considered relative to each other. This extension allows the internal structure of a change to be made explicit in a new way, bifurcating the change into yang parts and yin parts. I call this extended definition of change *bipolar change*.

  Links [Preprint] [Publication]

- Thread *exactphilosophy.net 2018 (1 Nov)* at the Usenet newsgroup alt.philosophy.taoism (Nov 2018).

  Links [Archive]

Shop

Books and more related to this website at artecat.ch:

With books that reproduce web pages and articles of this website as printed books, as well as as free PDF ebooks, plus books that bring specific subjects to hopefully a wider range of readers in accessible form, and in the future maybe 3D prints, posters, videos, and more. . .

Links

Yi Jing Algebra
Mathematical approaches to the I Ching, by Andreas Schöter.

Greek Elements
Detailed article by John Opsopaus; from ancient Greece to Jung.

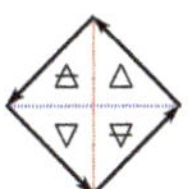

Energy Language
Images speaking about elementary cycles and more, by Billy Culver.

Four Elements
Inspiring book by John O'Donohue; breath, tears, hearth and sphinx.

Apocatastasis
Emil Lips' considerate synthesis of 'everything' from three dualities...

What is exactphilosophy?

This is the beginning of an article with the same title at exactphilosophy.net to maybe give you a glimpse of the "mindset" behind the new word or concept, which is not directly related to the society with a similar name:

A new word for the dictionary that I would define maybe like this:

exactphilosophy n.

A way of doing philosophy that aims at eventually producing scientific hypotheses, while avoiding internal inconsistencies (or making them explicit) and correcting factual errors whenever detected. It avoids to make things too specific unless they are carefully settled, influenced by ancient Asian traditions, especially by the Tao in Chinese philosophy, and by pataphysics. It could be imagined as floating around 'reality' like a magic carpet, while gently trying to settle down, with a care similar to the proverbial fox in China crossing a river on thin ice.

Note that this is about exactphilosophy in **one** word and **not** capitalized.

The adjective would be "exactphilosophical", the adverb "exactphilosophically", the verb "exactphilosophize". Privately, I often abbreviate exactphilosophy as "xphi" or even, more rarely, as "xφ".